A PRACTICAL GUIDE TO WINDOWS NT

KENNETH L. SPENCER

A PRACTICAL GUIDE TO WINDOWS NT

KENNETH L. SPENCER

CBM
BOOKS

Printed in the United States of America.

Trademark Acknowledgments

AXP, DECnet, Etherworks, NAS, Network Application Support, OpenVMS, Pathworks, Pathworks for Windows NT, Pathworks Links, Polycenter, and TeamLinks are trademarks of Digital Equipment Corp.

LaserJet and Precision Architecture are trademarks of Hewlett-Packard Co.

OS/2 is a trademark of IBM Corp.

Clipper is a trademark of Intergraph Corp.

Modular Windows, MS-DOS V5.0, MS-DOS V6.0, Windows for Workgroups, Windows NT, Windows NT Advanced Server, Windows Open Systems Architecture, Windows V3.1, Win32, Word for Windows, Workgroup Connection, and WOSA are trademarks of Microsoft Corp.

R4000 is a trademark of Mips Technologies Inc.

NetWare is a trademark of Novell Inc.

Sparcstation is a trademark of Sun Microsystems Inc.

UNIX is a registered trademark of UNIX System Laboratories

WinBatch is a trademark of Wilson WindowWare Inc.

EtherLink III is a trademark of 3Com Corp.

All other trademarks are the property of their respective owners.

Library of Congress Cataloging-in-Publication Data

Spencer, Kenneth L., 1951-
   A practical guide to Windows NT / Kenneth L. Spencer.
     p. cm.
   Includes index.
   ISBN 1-878956-39-6
   1. Operating systems (Computers) 2. Windows NT. I. Title.
QA76.76.063S67 1993
005.4'469—dc20   93-5418
                             CIP

Please address comments and questions to the publisher:
CBM Books
101 Witmer Road
Horsham, PA 19044
(215)957-1500 FAX(215)957-1050

Editor: Eric Schoeniger
Editorial Coordinator: Debbie Hiller
Production Manager: Patty Wall
Cover Design: Tom Owen

Contents

CHAPTER 2: THE WINDOWS NT COMMAND PROMPT

CHAPTER 3: WINDOWS NT PRINT SERVICES

CHAPTER 4: WINDOWS NT NETWORKING

CHAPTER 5: THE WINDOWS NT ARCHITECTURE

CHAPTER 8: EVENT VIEWER

CHAPTER 9: USER MANAGER

CHAPTER 10: WINDOWS NT SECURITY

Preface

THE WINDOWS NT PRODUCT

Microsoft Corp.'s Windows NT is a full-featured environment, extending the Windows product line into new markets and providing support for multiprocessor machines, non-Intel hardware platforms, and advanced networking. Windows NT is a member of the Windows family and will run all Windows V3.x applications. Microsoft has stated that all MS Server applications will be ported to Windows NT and that networks using NT as a server will coexist with LAN Manager network servers running IBM Corp.'s OS/2, UNIX, and Digital Equipment Corp.'s OpenVMS.

NT is a very powerful environment, supporting not only Windows, but POSIX and OS/2 applications as well. With the recent adoption by Digital of Windows and Windows applications into its Network Application Support (NAS) environment, NT becomes a strategic player in the Digital market, especially with the introduction of Pathworks Links, TeamLinks, and other Digital Windows products. Other vendors have jumped on the NT bandwagon, with support for NT a primary focus of their products. IBM even supports NT on its products, even though NT competes with OS/2.

Windows Open Systems Architecture

The Windows Open Services Architecture (WOSA) is Microsoft's map of the future for operating systems. It is a drastic departure from current trends because of the support for many application program interfaces (API) and the way it uses the graphical user interface (GUI) as the main operating system and the command line interface (that is, DOS) as a behind-the-scenes tool. WOSA defines the architecture for Windows over the next several years. NT is currently at the top of this architecture, with Modular Windows on the low end for consumer appliances.

The following diagram shows some of Microsoft's plans for the Windows architecture over the next 2 years.

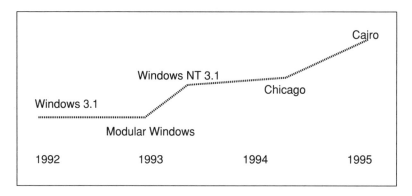

Windows NT is not the end of the road but the beginning of a new generation of Windows systems. Glimpses of the future Chicago product have given us a glimpse of the future version of Windows that will replace Windows V3.1. Cairo is the code name for a new version of NT that will appear around late 1994 or 1995. Each of these products will take us a step closer up the evolutionary path toward an ideal operating system.

Focus of This Book

This book is targeted at the vast majority of NT users and managers. Topics are geared to a level that most people will use, without being general enough to insult your intelligence but stopping short of the techno-babble that most systems people drop into. At times we will resort to techo-talk, but I have tried to keep it to a minimum.

Caveat Emptor

Buyer beware! How's that for honesty right off the bat?

This book was developed during the time period from the first NT beta (July 1992) to the last 30 to 60 days before the release of the final NT product. Many things changed in the product during this time period, and Microsoft made changes to the intended product configurations of the final product.

I have been as diligent as possible in keeping abreast of these changes and making sure that everything in the book is current. However, I am very sure that a few of the screen shots and one or two of the references refer to something that was changed.

If you find any of these items, I would appreciate an update with the reference and the problem. All notes on this subject should be sent to my attention at Cardinal Business Media.

Acknowledgments

I would like to thank my wife, Patricia, and my children, Ken Jr. and Jeffrey, for their support and help on this project. Writing about a system such as Windows NT takes a great deal of time and effort and a lot of support from your family when you are doing it in your spare time.

Brian Langenbach and Greg Griswold from Effective Management Systems also deserve a lot of thanks for their help. They both reviewed the manuscript and contributed from a technical perspective. Their experience with both NT and other systems such as DOS, Windows V3.1, UNIX, and OpenVMS was very helpful.

Joe Catalanotti also deserves special mention for his help from a Digital Equipment perspective. Joe was instrumental in providing me with copies of Pathworks for Windows NT and other information from Digital. Joe is one of those rare individuals who can work within the corporate world and get things done where others seem to spin their wheels.

Steve Harvey is a super friend who has provided support during this project and always had time for counseling me on the correct approach. Steve has a special insight into products like NT and what makes them valuable to the corporate world.

CHAPTER 1

Using Windows NT

INTRODUCTION TO THE NT INTERFACE

The Windows NT user interface (with the Windows API) has the same look and feel of Windows V3.1 and later. Most users will not be able to tell the difference in using NT or V3.x when using their favorite applications. Cut and paste, Dynamic Data Exchange (DDE), Object Linking and Embedding (OLE), and other traditional Windows features will work fine with NT.

This chapter reviews most of the Windows features that people will use in their day-to-day activities. Many of these programs share the look and feel of their Windows V3.x counterparts. I will not try to cover every possible feature of each program but will instead concentrate on the new and changed features, especially features that add to the functionality and usability of NT.

Accessing Windows

The log on/log off process presents the biggest difference a user will face in using NT versus Windows V3.x. A user must successfully log on to NT before NT will allow access to any system services, such as programs or disks. The logon process is similar to logging on to any other secure system in which the user gains access to the system by supplying a valid username and password.

Logging On and Off of NT

After an NT system is booted, it will display a screen requesting you to log on by pressing Ctrl+Alt+Del, the same key sequence used to warm-boot a normal DOS PC. This may seem a little unsettling, but it simply causes NT to load the logon dialog box, which prompts the user for a username and password. The following figure illustrates the Welcome dialog.

Welcome Dialog

You can also log on to NT from within an NT session by selecting File/Logoff or pressing Ctrl+Alt+Del and selecting Logoff. Either one of these actions will cause NT to display the Welcome dialog, allowing you an opportunity to log on. The following figure shows the NT Security Dialog, which is displayed after pressing Ctrl+Alt+Del from an active NT session.

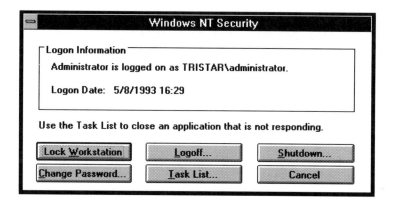

Windows NT Security Dialog

The program manager is displayed after the logon process is completed. From this point on, NT looks and behaves like a traditional Windows system.

The Logoff function is the complement to the logon process. Logoff replaces the traditional Exit command found on Windows V3.x systems and is accessed in the same manner (from the File menu or by pressing Alt-F4). The File menu is shown below.

Program Manager File Menu

The following dialog is displayed after Logoff is selected.

Logoff Dialog

This is the old, familiar exiting Windows dialog that we are used to from V3.x. The only difference is that NT will log you off and redisplay the NT Security dialog.

Changing Your Password
NT will prompt you at login to change your password after it expires. Simply key in your new password, key it in again to verify that you typed it correctly, and click OK. That's all there is to it.

You can also change your password during an NT session. Members of the Power Users or Administrators group can use User Manager to change their own and others' passwords. Select the user to change and display the user properties dialog by double-clicking the user account. Change the password and confirm it in the appropriate fields.

All users have access to the NT Security dialog. The Security dialog is accessed by pressing Ctl+Alt+Del any time during an NT session. One of the option buttons is Change Password. Click this button, enter the new password, and confirm. Popping up the Security dialog is the quickest way to change your password during a session. You cannot change another user's password with the Security dialog.

WINDOWS QUICK TIPS

The Windows GUI provides a time-tested and easy-to-use interface. Some features of the interface may seem strange (why double-click an icon?) but actually adhere to the Common User Access (CUA) specification produced by IBM. The CUA is a standard that specifies how a program should look and operate. The Windows Quick Tips section will not exhaustively cover the CUA but will cover the basics of getting around Windows. If you are an experienced Windows user, you can skip this section.

Double-Click or Single-Click?

The double-click/single-click enigma has puzzled a large number of users. Why do we have to double-click an icon in Program Manager but single-click an option on the

Word for Windows toolbar? This troubling paradox is at the heart of many Windows interface issues.

Windows provides the double-click short cut almost anywhere that you must select an option from a list or group and then click OK. Double-clicking the option will perform both events simultaneously. Program Manager icons are executed by clicking and pressing Enter or double-clicking.

Most Windows programs use a single click to execute options from within the program via toolbars or groups of icons. Double-clicking is still used for selecting options from list boxes.

Selecting Items

Selecting an item in Windows means to highlight the item (turn the item black) in preparation for performing some task, such as deleting a word or sentence or choosing multiple items in File Manager. The following table covers the most common selection methods.

Method	Selects
Click Once	Select an icon, button, check box, menu option, or item in a list box.
Double-Click a Word	Select an entire word. Click again on another word, and the words in between it and the original will be added to the selection.
Click and Select	Click and hold down the left button, move the mouse to the end of your selection, and release. This will be added to the selection.
Arrow Key	Moving an arrow key in some applications will move the selection to the next option (Program Manager).
Tab Key	The tab key moves between options in a form or group of buttons.
Space Bar	Pressing the space bar when a command button or option button is selected will execute the command or turn on the option button.

Cursors to the Rescue

Windows has always had a penchant for different types of cursors. The dreaded hourglass cursor has been around for ages to indicate just how slow our hardware is when running a monster like Windows. NT introduces a new twist to the hourglass.

New NT Cursor

This new cursor indicates when an application is busy performing a task. It is similar to the old hourglass but has a new twist: You don't have to quit working while the application is busy. For instance, if you kickoff a large print job in Word, this cursor may appear. Press Alt+Tab and switch to print manager or any other application, even if Word was running full-screen.

You will still see the old, familiar hourglass cursor in some applications. NT will usually behave the same when this cursor is displayed as with the new cursor.

Hint: When you click on an option and see the new cursor, but the option does not seem to be executing, be patient. This is usually because an application must be loaded from disk, which can take several seconds. Quickly double-clicking the option again will usually start two copies of the program or trigger errors in the application. Check out the cursor function in the Control Panel.

Drag and Drop

Windows drag-and-drop capabilities are used by many applications to allow you to quickly move or copy one or more items to another location or to add or remove an item from a group or list. For instance, Program Manager allows you to drag a program item from one group and drop it into another group. You can perform the same action by pressing F8 and selecting the group, but drag and drop feels more intuitive. The drag-and-drop operation is one of the simplest functions in Windows:

1. Click on the object.
2. Continue to hold down the left mouse button.
3. Drag the object over its target.
4. Release the mouse button.

File Manager is another application that makes extensive use of drag and drop. Did you know that you can drag an item in File Manager and drop it in a Program Manager group? This action is the same as going through File New in Program Manager to create a new program item icon. Drag and drop is also used by User Manager to add users to or remove users from groups.

Another popular use of drag and drop is to embed objects in another application. For instance, let's say you need to place a picture in a Word for Windows document.

One of the fastest ways to accomplish this is to drag the file of the graphic and drop it over the word document. This will deposit the graphic in the Word document.

Many commercial applications are adding drag-and-drop functionality. Check out the new features in updates for your favorite application. Pay special attention to drag and drop, because some drag-and-drop options are not obvious at first glance.

Switching Between Applications

The Windows interface provides two ways to switch between applications. The standard method has been to press Ctrl+Esc to bring up the Task List. The Task menu will contain a list of all the applications that are currently executing. Double-click an application, and you will switch to it immediately. You can also select the application and click Switch To. The Task List can also be displayed by double-clicking on an area of the screen that does not contain an application or program manager.

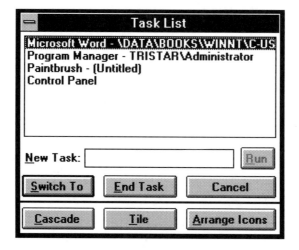

Task List Dialog

There are several buttons on the Task List dialog. The first two buttons act on the application in the list that is selected (highlighted), while the buttons on the bottom act on running applications.

Button	Description
Switch To	Switch to the selected application.
End Task	End (terminate) the selected application.
Cancel	Close the task list.
Cascade	Cascade all running applications.
Tile	Tile all running applications.
Arrange Icons	Arrange the icons of minimized applications across the bottom of the desktop.
Run	Run a program.

Notice that the Task List now includes an option to run another program. You can run any program that will run under NT, including Win32, Win16, DOS, OS/2, and other applications supported by NT. Simply enter the name of the application and click Run. The application must be located somewhere in the NT path, the current directory, or the default NT directory (WINNT), unless you enter the full path to the program.

Another way to quickly switch to another application is via the Alt+Tab combination. The trick is to hold down the Alt key and press and release the Tab key. Each time you press the Tab key, NT will display a small box showing the application name. When you see the name of the application you want to switch to, release the Alt key, and viola, you're there. You can cancel the operation when another program box is displayed by pressing the Esc key before you release Alt.

Menus

Most programs offer pull-down menu access to commands and options. Click on the menu name at the top of the screen to display any menu. A menu in Windows is sticky: When you click its title, it drops down and stays until you select an option. You can also use the hot key to display a menu. Hot keys are indicated by the underlined key in the menu name. Press Alt+Letter (Letter = Underlined key) and the menu will display.

To select a menu option, click the option once. The up and down arrow keys can also be used to move the highlight bar up and down the menu. Notice in the following options menu that menus also have hot keys. You could quickly access the Options menu (shown below) by pressing Alt+O and then selecting the Minimize on Use option by pressing O (O = hot key).

Most Windows menus contain commands that perform tasks or display dialog boxes for setting Windows options. Some menus will also contain options that may be turned on or off. The check marks can be seen on the Options menu shown below; the menu is from File Manager.

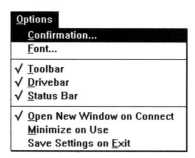

Sample Options Menu

Windows also has a standard set of menus that may or may not appear in both Windows and Windows application programs. These menus are listed below.

Menu Name	Description
File	The File (or first menu option) usually contains major tasks for the program. For instance, Disk Manager has a Partition menu. Commands to exit the program will also be found on the first menu.
Edit	Provides access to Windows clipboard functions (cut, copy, and paste). Options will also exist that are specific to the program.
Options	The Options menu usually has selections that determine how the program operates.
Window	A Window menu is used by programs that typically display multiple windows. Options on the Window menu usually allow you to control the location of the windows and switch from one window to another.
Help	Most programs will have a Help menu that provides direct access to the Help subsystems.

Control Menu

The Control menu is available from almost every Windows program by pressing Alt+Space or clicking the small box in the top-left corner of the window (the box with the long dash in the middle). The Control menu is an NT system service that automatically appears on each programs window unless it has been disabled by the application. Application programs may turn off the menu by calling an NT API function or setting options in the program.

The format of the Control menu is usually the same in each program, unless you have installed programs such as the HDC tools or the ever-popular Winbatch system from Wilson WindowWare. These programs attach themselves to the Control menu and provide quick access to almost any other program. The standard Control menu is shown below.

Control Menu

Some application programs may add functions to the Control menu. This was a popular thing to do in the early days of Windows but is not done very often now. The Control menu was handy when lots of people tried to use Windows without a mouse (how else would you resize or minimize a window?) but is primarily used to close an application now.

Notice in the graphic that Alt+F4 is a shortcut to close the application. Alt+F4 is available in most applications for this purpose. Double-clicking the Control menu is another way to quickly close an application.

PROGRAM MANAGER

Program Manager will be the main interface with NT for most users. Program Manager provides a simple interface for selecting a program. Programs are stored in groups and can be executed by double-clicking a program's icon or clicking an icon and pressing enter.

The NT Program Manager has not changed much from Windows V3.1 . The appearance and function is the same as in a V3.x system, except for the way NT handles program groups and preferences and several other options. There is also a slight change in appearance because of the personal or common group indicator on each group; at the bottom of the figure below, notice the single head for personal groups and the computer icon for common groups. NT will display different groups and maintain preferences for each user account. This allows NT to control access to different programs and program groups and protect preference changes from affecting other users. Chapters 5 and 6 include more information about Program Manager groups and preferences.

Program Manager shows the system and user account names in the title bar. The Program Manager screen is shown below.

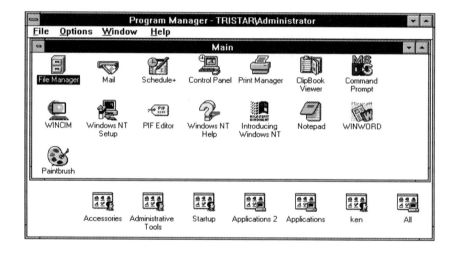

Program Manager

The File New command brings up a dialog box that allows you to select whether program item or group changes are for all users or just for the current user. You must be a member of the Administrators or Power Users group to change the global settings.

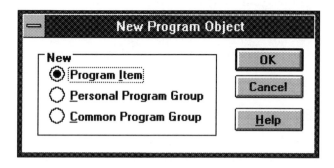

New Program Object Dialog

The functions of the new box are shown below.

Option	Description
Program Item	Displays the standard dialog for adding a program item to a group.
Personal Program Group	Adds the file or group for only the current user.
Common Program Group	Adds the item or group for every user.

The Options menu has also changed slightly in NT. There is a super new option that allows you to save preferences immediately, alleviating the need to remember to hold down the shift key and click on File Exit as in Windows V3.1.

The Auto Arrange option is turned on in the graphic of the menu below. This causes NT to automatically arrange the items in a program group when they are changed. This is handy when you add a new program or move a program. If this option is not checked, you must manually arrange program icons each time you move an icon.

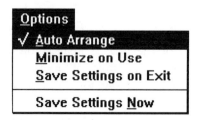

Program Manager Options Menu

The Save Settings on Exit option causes NT to save preference settings each time you log off. This option is dangerous and should be turned off. Leaving this option on will cause NT to save your Program Manager preferences every time you log off. This means that if you accidentally move something or change another option, those changes will be saved. I like to have my program groups and applications in the same place when I log in. It's no fun poking around all the program groups looking for them.

FILE MANAGER OVERVIEW

File Manager is one of the Windows programs with the most enhancements in NT. The interface and function is basically the same as that found in the Windows for Workgroups product. The following figure shows the File Manager main window.

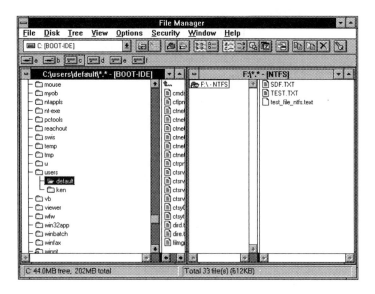

File Manager

The only major appearance changes to File Manager are the additional menu option (Security) and the addition of the new toolbar below the menu. The toolbar is designed to provide quick access to a number of functions, and its operation is almost identical to that of the toolbar in Windows for Workgroups. You will quickly become accustomed to using the toolbar and wish it had room for more buttons. The next figure shows the toolbar and labels several of the standard toolbar buttons.

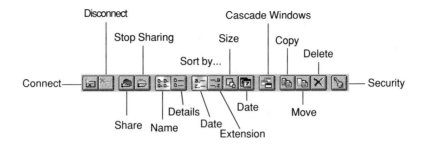

File Manager Toolbar

The toolbar functions include standard features from Windows V3.x and new features specific to NT. The Connect, Disconnect, Share, and Stop Sharing buttons are network functions for connecting to and sharing directory resources. The other buttons are for controlling the appearance of the File Manager windows and managing files. You can also customize the toolbar using the Options/Customize Toolbar option.

The new File Manager functions are primarily concerned with accessing file and print services and managing the security of your file system. This includes offering local services to be shared over the network and accessing shared services located on other systems. Additional services are provided for managing security of NT File System (NTFS) volumes. Other minor features deal with controlling the display of File Manager windows. Each of these features is explained below, except for the security features, which are covered in Chapter 9.

Network and Disk Functions

Network and disk functions are tucked away under the Disk menu. Drive selections are also available through the drop-down list at the left end of the toolbar.

The functions at the top of the menu are related strictly to local disk functions. Copy Disk will copy a floppy disk, just like the DISKCOPY DOS function. Label Disk will display a dialog allowing you to change the label of a disk. Format Floppy will format a floppy disk.

File Manager File Menu

The File menu has added options for connecting/disconnecting network services and sharing/stop sharing services. These new functions perform the same functions as the corresponding buttons on the toolbar. Each of these functions is covered later in this chapter under the Sharing Resources and Connecting to Shared Resources sections.

Setting File Manager Options

The Options menu is used to select options that control how File Manager functions and the appearance of File Manager windows. Some of the features, such as Confirmation, are similar to those of the Windows V3.x File Manager, while others are totally new, such as Open New Window on Connect. Notice that in addition to the standard functions, this menu has options to turn on or off the display of the Toolbar, Drivebar, and Status Bar. The check mark indicates that the option is turned on, while the absence of the check mark indicates that the option is turned off.

```
Options
  Confirmation...
  Font...
  Customize Toolbar...
  √ Toolbar
  √ Drivebar
  √ Status Bar
  √ Open New Window on Connect
  Minimize on Use
  Save Settings on Exit
```

File Manager Options Menu

The Open New Window on Connect feature can also be turned on or off. Turning this option on causes File Manager to display a new File menu whenever you connect to a shared file resource. This is a nice feature to turn on when you are doing a lot of file maintenance, such as moving files or directories across several drives or directory structures. You may want to turn this off during normal operations when you may not want to automatically pop up a new file window with each connection. Turning this option off will also speed up your connect time, because File Manager does not have to read and display the directory entries for each new connection.

Using File Manager Windows

File Manager uses a separate window for each drive it displays. A drive window is normally separated into two panes: one for the directories and one for the files in the current directory. You can also have many windows open at the same time. Multiple windows are particularly helpful for moving files around on your system, especially in a network environment. Open one window that contains the files to move and another with the target directory structure. Drag the files over the target and drop them on the target directory. You can quickly move entire disk structures in this manner. See the next section of this chapter for more information about files in File Manager.

The Window menu controls the file windows in File Manager. It includes the standard arrange functions: Tile, Cascade, and Arrange Icons, plus an option for creating a new window. The Tile options provide the ability to tile the windows vertically or horizontally, instead of just horizontally. The vertical option was present in Windows V3.1, but was accessible only by holding down the Shift key and then clicking Window/Tile.

File Manager Window Menu

You can also create a new window by double-clicking on a drive icon. This will display a new default file window over the other file windows.

The Refresh option is handy for updating the display of File Manager when a program changes the status of a drive that File Manager is unaware of. This can occur from a command prompt program or sometimes from an application program. Selecting File Manager and pressing F5 will quickly update the current drive window.

ACCESSING AND USING FILES

The heart of any computer operating system is the resources and tools it provides for accessing file resources. NT provides the standard Windows tools in File Manager and the command prompt applications that are familiar to DOS and Windows V3.x users. NT also brings along two new file systems: NTFS and High-Performance File System (HPFS). Chapter 5 offers additional information about the file systems.

NT's support for other operating environments adds a lot of power to the use of its file systems. A UNIX command shell will add the power of the rich set of UNIX file and script commands to the standard NT commands (see Chapter 2). These types of tools can greatly extend the management capabilities of your file system.

The NT File Manager provides the same drop-and-drag features for accessing files that the Windows V3.1 File Manager does. The following list provides a few of the shortcuts for manipulating files; for more information about the basic functions within File Manager, consult the NT documentation or any of the popular Windows books:

◆ To copy a file, click the filename and drag the file to its new location. If the file is being copied to a location on the same disk, hold down the Ctrl key when you select the file.

◆ To move a file, click the filename and drag the file to its new location. If the file is being moved to a different disk, hold down the Shift key while selecting the file.

◆ To copy a file to the clipboard, select the file and select File/Copy to Clipboard.

SHARING RESOURCES

Setting up and sharing resources over the network has never been easier than with NT. Sharable resources are either file or print resources. When a resource is shared over the network, any user with the correct security can connect to it. The graphical interface of File Manager and Print Manager is used to select the resources to share and specify the share parameters.

Share and Stop Sharing Buttons

The Share (left button) and Stop Sharing (right button) toolbar buttons are used to share and unshare resources over the network. The same functions are available under the File menu (File Manager) and Print menu (Print Manager). The steps to share a resource are very simple:

1. Select the printer, drive or directory to share.

2. Click on the share icon.

3. Enter the share parameters, if any.

4. Click OK.

The New Share dialog is shown below.

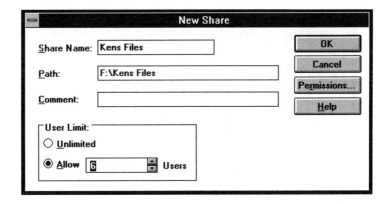

New Share Dialog

As soon a resource is shared, it will become visible to other users on the network that are running NT-compatible systems. This includes Windows for Workgroups, LAN Manager clients, and NT. Remember that other systems must be using the same network protocol to connect to your NT system resources. For instance, a LAN Manager client running Digital's DECnet cannot connect to a plain NT system that is using NetBEUI. If you use DECnet on both systems, viola, they can connect.

NT provides several options in the share dialog for controlling how the resource is shared. The options are listed below.

Option	Description
Share Name	The Share Name field contains the name that will be displayed as the share name over the network. The default name is the path name.
Path	The Path field must contain the full path name of the resource to share.
Comment	This field can be used for a comment that will be displayed whenever the share name is displayed over the network.
User Limit	The User Limit field can be used to limit the number of users that may simultaneously connect to a resource.
Permissions	The Permissions button will display the Permissions dialog, allowing you to select permissions for the shared resource.

You may see the following dialog when sharing NTFS directories. This is a warning that some MS-DOS systems may not be able to access the files on the shared resource.

Share Warning for MS-DOS Clients

NT also provides command line options of the NET utilities for sharing resources. NET SHARE can be used interactively at the command prompt or in a command file to connect to shared resources. This command is useful when you need to connect to a network resource during a batch program, use the resource and then disconnect from the resource. Chapter 2 offers more information about NET SHARE and other command line options. Entering /? after any command will display options for the command.

The Stop Sharing button will display a dialog that allows you to select the resource to stop sharing. When you stop sharing a network disk, the resource becomes unavailable to other users on the network. If anyone is using the resource when sharing is terminated, he or she will be disconnected.

Chapter 6 offers more information about sharing resources.

CONNECTING TO SHARED RESOURCES

NT resources (directories and printers) can be accessed by any NT-compatible system on the network. NT workstations can also connect to any shared resource on an NT-compatible system on the network, including Pathworks servers, Novell NetWare servers, Windows for Workgroups workstations, and many others. Some servers, such as Pathworks and NetWare, will require adding drivers to an NT workstation before NT can access resources on these servers. Others, such as Windows for Workgroups, do not require any special software.

NT provides access to shared resources through the Connect/Disconnect buttons on the File Manager toolbar. The following graphic illustrates the Connect (left button) and Disconnect (right button) buttons.

Connect and Disconnect Buttons

Clicking the Connect button will display the Connect dialog. This dialog allows you to connect to a resource by entering the Path name or clicking on the resource in the Shared Directories list box.

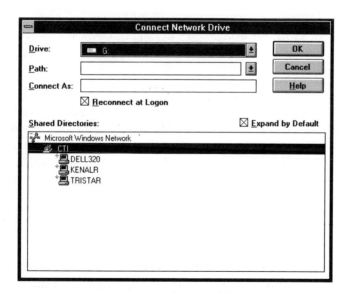

File Manager Connect Network Drive Dialog

The Connect Network Drive dialog supports the browsing of network resources. The Browse function queries other systems on the network and displays the shared resources in a list. The user can browse the list until the desired resource is displayed. Once the desired resource is displayed, a couple of mouse clicks completes the task.

Double-clicking on a workgroup will display all the workstations in that workgroup. Clicking on a particular workstation displays all the shared resources under that workstation. Notice how this dialog shows the network name as Microsoft Windows Network. The workgroup name (CTI) is listed just below. The DELL320 and KENALR machines are running Windows for Workgroups, while the TRI-STAR is the NT machine. Can't tell the difference between them, can you?

The steps for connecting to a shared resource by browsing are:

1. Click on the Connect button.

2. Select the drive letter to use for the resource.

3. Click on the Workgroup (if not displayed).

4. Click on the desired workstation.

5. Click on the shared resource.

6. Click OK.

The Expand by Default check box causes File Manager to expand the display to include all computers in the workgroup or domain. Click the check box to turn it off. Leaving this on may slow down the display of the dialog if you have lots of systems on your network.

Connecting to a service by entering the service name requires that you know the name of the server and the service that you wish to connect to. Accessing resources on another network such as a Pathworks V4.x server is an example of a server that does not have browsing capabilities allowing client workstations to choose from a list of shared server resources. To connect to a server that does not allow browsing, you must enter the full Universal Naming Convention (UNC) name of the resource you wish to connect to.

This process is essentially the same as the one you use for Windows V3.1 to connect to a system that does not allow browsing.

NT also provides command line options of the NET utilities for connecting to shared resources. NET USE can be used interactively at the command prompt or in a command file to connect to shared resources. This command is useful when you need to connect to a network resource during a batch program, use the resource and then disconnect from the resource. Chapter 2 offers more information about NET USE and other command line options. Entering /? after any command will display options for the command.

Connecting to shared print resources uses the same process as file resources. The Connect to Print Resources dialog also contains useful information about the status of the printer to which you are connecting. For more information about using network printers, see Chapter 3.

WINDOWS PROGRAMS UNDER NT

Running a Windows program under NT is just like running a program under Windows V3.x. The interaction of the program with itself and other programs will be the same, with two big exceptions.

First, the program may run faster. This is because NT can run on much more powerful machines than V3.1 and NT uses the Win32 API. Win32 is a 32-bit API for the NT operating system and its commands are more powerful and efficient than the Windows V3.x 16-bit API.

Second, NT is a truly multitasking operating system. This is a visible improvement over Windows V3.1 because you can switch between applications at any time. For example, let's say you have a large Word document that you have just sent to the printer under Windows V3.1. The dreaded hourglass displays and you know that it will be there for 5 minutes. Further, unless you have remembered to shrink Word from its maximized mode, you can't switch to anything! Ctrl+Esc will work only when Word has completed sending the job to the printer. Pressing Ctrl+Esc under NT will pop the task list immediately, no matter which state Word is in! This is because of NT's pre-emptive multitasking.

When you pressed Ctrl+Esc, you pre-empted NT from the task it was performing and said, "Hey, I want control." From the task list you can switch to any other application and continue working until Word has finished sending the job to the printer.

Pre-emptive multitasking also feels faster than Windows V3.x, particularly when you are running multiple applications at the same time. NT can run several applications that are performing tasks, such as sorting, calculations, or macros, with very little performance degradation. NT will really fly when running on one of the new multiprocessor machines.

Common NT/Windows for Workgroups Programs

NT includes a number of applications that are the same as or very similar to applications that first shipped with Windows for Workgroups: Chat, Mail, Schedule+, and

ClipBook Viewer. The NT versions of these programs are Win32 applications that make use of the Win32 API and, therefore, NT's full architecture. Each of these programs is a network-capable program that works equally well with other NT and Windows for Workgroups workstations on a network.

This chapter provides a brief look at the Chat, Mail, and Schedule+ applications. For a more in-depth review of the programs included with NT and detailed instructions on each program, refer to the NT documentation and the help files for each application.

Chat

Chat is a neat little program that provides NT users with the ability to interactively talk with another network user running Chat on a Windows for Workgroups or NT workstation. Chat does not need a lot of explanation or detailed information about how to use the program. The following graphic provides a view of the Chat window and the two panes for communicating between users.

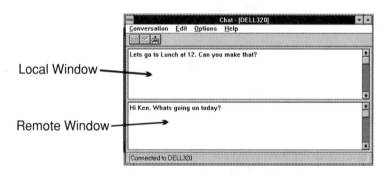

Chat Window

Chat is very easy to use. The following table shows the three icons in the toolbar and a quick description of their use.

Icon	Description
	Clicking this icon allows you to call another workstation.
	A click of this icon will answer a call from another workstation. You can also answer a call by double-clicking the ringing Chat icon on the desktop.
	Clicking this icon will hang up a conversation between you and another usage.

You can also explore the Options menu, which provides options for setting preferences, fonts, colors, and whether you want the toolbar or status bar display. Chat also allows you to arrange the window panes in horizontal or vertical fashion and turn sound on or off.

Mail

The NT Mail program is a member of the Microsoft Mail family. It will interoperate with Windows for Workgroups, NT workstations, and a number of other mail systems and networks. The interface to mail is intuitive and easy to use. The next figure shows the main Mail window.

The Mail interface is neatly organized, using a row of large buttons across the top and Multiple Document Interface (MDI) windows within the main Mail window. Within the Main window you can use folders to store your messages. Folders can also contain other folders, providing a nice tool for organizing your messages. Each open folder is displayed in its own window. You double-click on a folder to open it. Once open, a folder can be resized or minimized. The following figure shows the main Mail window with the Inbox displayed.

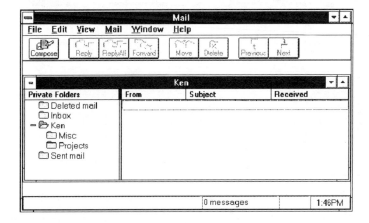

Main Mail Window

One of Mail's features I really like is the ability to minimize a folder, including the Inbox and Outbox. I usually open several windows, one for each of my most popular folders, and then minimize each window. Then I use the Window/Auto Arrange option to neatly arrange the row of icons along the bottom of the window. The following figure shows the icons for several minimized windows.

Minimized Mail Icons

The style of the icon shows the type of window. The left icon is a note that has not been completed. The next icon is a minimized folder named Ken. The last two icons show the outbox and inbox. Using icons for folders allows me to quickly open any folder by double-clicking the folder.

You can also display the Inbox and Outbox at the same time by selecting Window/ Tile, as shown in the next figure.

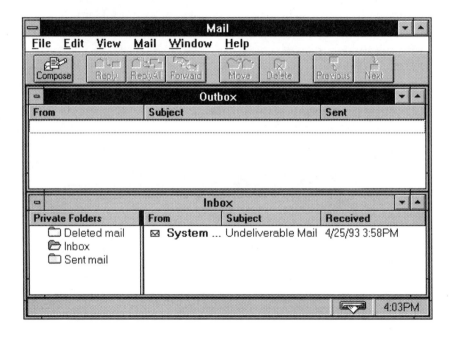

Mail with Tiled Windows

Another nice feature of the Mail interface is the hot headers. For instance, in the Inbox, click on Private Folders to display the Shared Folders. Click on Shared Folders to display Private Folders. You can also click From, Subject, and Received to sort the messages by that column. The Outbox messages can also be sorted by clicking on From, Subject, or Sent To.

Creating a note in Mail is easy:

1. Click Compose.

2. Address the note.

3. Enter the message.

4. Click Send.

The next figure shows the compose dialog.

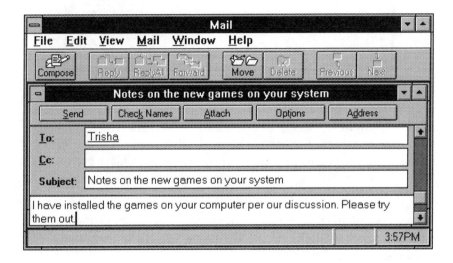

Mail Compose Dialog

Another neat feature of Mail is the Message Finder. Click the File Menu/Message Finder option, and the finder dialog will let you fill in search criteria for messages that you wish to look for.

Using the Message Finder is a fill-in-the-blank process in which you fill in the fields you wish to look for and start the search by clicking Start. The Where to Look option allows you to select the folders to search, reducing the volume of information to look through and reducing the search time.

There are lots of other features in Mail. If you are going to manage a Mail system, you need to spend a fair amount of time with the NT documentation on Mail. You should also experiment with Mail and test its various options.

You should also check out the Mail Postoffice Manager option. This application provides tools for managing and adding Mail users and managing Shared Folders.

The following figure shows the main window for the Postoffice Manager.

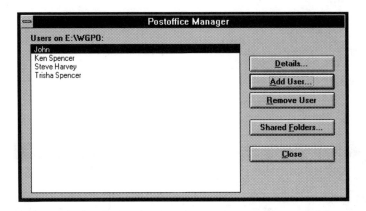

Mail Postoffice Manager Dialog

Mail allows you automate logging in to Mail by placing your user account name and password on the command line that starts mail. If you set up your icon or program this way, Mail will automatically log you in when you start mail, bypassing the login dialog.

Most security-conscious people will choke at the thought of placing a username and especially a password on the command line to start a program. Doing this in Program Manager means that anyone accessing the properties of the icon used for Mail can obtain your username and password.

You can minimize this problem by placing the Mail icon in a personal group instead of a common group. This will restrict access to the Properties dialog to the user of the account, as long as the user does not leave the workstation logged in when he or she leaves the area. You can also improve the security of your users by having them lock their workstation whenever they leave. You can automate the lock-workstation feature by checking the Password Protected box on the Screen Savers dialog in Control Panel. A password-protected screen saver forces anyone trying to access the system to use the original login password to gain access.

Schedule+

NT's Schedule+ application is the Win32 version of Schedule+ that ships with Windows for Workgroups. As with other NT applications, Schedule+ will work with systems running NT and Windows for Workgroups.

Schedule+ is designed for managing calendars in a workgroup or standalone workstation. You can create schedules with appointments such as meetings and other events.

If you are using Schedule+ on a network, you can automatically schedule meetings with other people, including sending automatic notification of the meeting and checking the other attendees' calendars.

Schedule+ also allows you to work online using the schedule files on your network or offline using the schedule files on your local workstation. Working offline is great for people who travel because you can take your schedule with you on your notebook. When you return to the office, schedule plus will merge the changes made offline with your online files.

The next figure shows the main Schedule+ window. Notice the two minimized icons for Ken's schedule and an Inbox for new messages.

Main Schedule+ Window

Schedule+ uses Mail for many of its functions and will not run if it can't find the Mail components it needs. When you start Schedule+, it will ask you for your password. This password is the Mail password for your user account.

Schedule+ must be running to receive notification of reminders that you have set. If you are going to use Schedule+ on a regular basis, you should start it in your Startup group to ensure that it is running whenever you login. You should not use the File/ Exit And Sign Out option unless you are sure you want to shut down Schedule+.

Schedule+ allows you to enter appointments in your schedule for normal events and recurring events. A recurring event is an event that occurs at specific intervals over time, for example, a meeting every Friday at 8:00 a.m.

CHAPTER 2

The Windows NT Command Prompt

INTRODUCTION TO THE NT COMMAND PROMPT

The NT command prompt is the character interface for NT systems. The command prompt supports running any application supported by NT, including batch commands (.CMD and .BAT), WIIN16 or WIN32, MS-DOS, OS/2 V1.x, and POSIX programs.

The NT command prompt is very different from the old DOS command prompt. It may look the same and run the same programs, but the similarity stops there. There are new commands and new options on some familiar DOS V5.0 commands.

The NT command prompt can also run Windows programs! For example, to start Word for Windows from the prompt:

```
C:\> WINWORD
```

The command prompt includes built-in DOSKEY support for recalling and editing commands and building command macros. The command prompt has the Windows V3.1 look and feel, so users should feel right at home. Like the Windows V3.1 command prompt, the window can be resized, moved, maximized to full screen, and minimized. NT also introduces several new parameters for controlling commands.

When you look under the covers of the command prompt, you begin to recognize the power that lurks in the new options. NT has introduced several new general-purpose native commands and a number of network commands. Many of the network commands were inherited from LAN Manager and TCP/IP systems.

Let's take a look at the commands that NT supports. The following tables are organized into groupings by command category. After the tables, we will look at several examples of NT commands and how they are used.

Native NT Commands

Command	Description
AT	AT can schedule commands and programs for execution at a specific date and time.
ATTRIB	The ATTRIB command displays or changes a file's attributes.
BREAK	This command sets or clears Ctrl-C checking.
CALL	The CALL command is used in a batch program to execute another batch program.
CHCP	This command displays or sets the active code page.
CHDIR (CD)	The CD command changes the current directory.
CLS	CLS clears the screen (command prompt window).
CMD	CMD.EXE replaces the old familiar COMAND.COM as the NT command processor.
COMP	COMP compares the contents of files.
CONVERT	CONVERT converts a DOS (FAT) or OS/2 (HPFS) file system to NTFS.
COPY	The COPY command copies files to another location (disk or directory).
DATE	DATE displays or sets the current system date.
DEL	DEL deletes a file or group of files. The NT DEL command has some new features from the DOS V5.0 command.
DIR	The DIR command displays directories of files. The NT DIR command has some new features from the DOS V5.0 command.
DISKCOMP	DISKCOMP compares two disks and displays the differences. The /1 and /8 switches from DOS V5.0 are not supported.
DISKCOPY	The DISKCOPY command makes a duplicate diskette. The /1 switch from DOS V5.0 is not supported.
DOSKEY	DOSKEY support is built into the NT command prompt. This allows editing and recalling previous commands and creating macros.

ECHO	The ECHO command is used to display messages from command programs and to turn the automatic display of commands on or off.
ENDLOCAL	Used in batch programs to end localization of environment changes.
ERASE	Same as DEL.
EXIT	EXIT closes the command prompt window.
FC	FC compares files and displays the differences.
FIND	This command searches a file or group of files for a text string.
FINDSTR	FINDSTR is used to search for strings in text files.
FOR	The FOR command executes a command for each file within a set.
FORMAT	FORMAT is used to format diskettes and fixed disk drives. Switches /b, /s, and /u from DOS V5.0 are not supported. Format does support the new 2.8-MB floptical drive.
GOTO	GOTO is used in command programs to transfer control to a label within the program.
GRAFTABL	GRAFTABL enables the display of extended characters in graphics mode.
HELP	The HELP command provides information about NT commands.
IF	IF is used only within command programs to perform conditional checks.
KEYBD	KEYBD is used to configure a keyboard for a specific language.
LABEL	LABEL is used to create, change, or delete volume labels. New symbols (^ and &) can be used in volume labels.
MKDIR (MD)	MD is used to create new directories.
MODE	MODE is used to configure system devices.
MORE	MORE displays information from a text file one screen at a time. You can also use a pipe to supply information to MORE.

MOVE	MOVE is similar to the COPY command, except that it actually moves the file, deleting the original. Files can be moved only on the same drive.
PATH	PATH displays or sets the search path. A path can now be updated at the command prompt by specifying %PATH%.
POPD	POPD changes to the last directory set with PUSHD.
PRINT	PRINT prints a text file in the background. The following switches are not supported: /b, /u, /m, /s, /q, /t, /c, and /p.
PROMPT	The PROMPT command is used to change the display format of the NT command prompt.
PUSHD	Stores the current directory for later use by POPD and changes to the specified directory.
RECOVER	Can be used to recover files from a bad disk.
REM	REM flags lines as comments in batch programs and CONFIG.SYS.
RENAME (REN)	REN renames a file or group of files.
REPLACE	This command replaces files.
RESTORE	RESTORE is used to restore files from a backup disk made with BACKUP.
RMDIR (RM)	RM is used to delete a directory.
SET	SET displays or sets NT environment variables.
SETLOCAL	SETLOCAL is used in command programs only to begin the localization of environment changes.
SHIFT	SHIFT is used in command programs only to shift the position of replaceable parameters (see FOR).
SORT	The SORT command sorts data and can sort files of unlimited size.
START	The START command can be used to run a program in a new command prompt window.
SUBST	SUBST associates a particular path with a drive letter.
TIME	The TIME command displays or sets the system time.

TITLE	TITLE is used to display the windows title in the Title Bar.
TREE	TREE displays a graphical view of the directory structure.
TYPE	This command displays a file.
VER	VER displays the NT version.
VERIFY	VERIFY turns on verification of writes to disk files. This causes NT to verify that disk writes are successful.
VOL	VOL displays the disk volume label and serial number.
XCOPY	XCOPY copies files. It is normally faster and offers more options than COPY.

New Symbols

&&	The && symbol causes the following command to run only if the preceding command is successful.
&	& can be used to separate multiple commands on the same line.
||	The || symbol causes the following command to run only if the preceding command fails.
()	() is used to group commands.
^	This is the escape character.

SC Network Commands

NET ACCOUNTS	This command displays or sets logon and password requirements of servers in a domain.
NET COMPUTER	NET COMPUTER adds computers to domains.
NET CONFIG	Displays the controllable services that are running.
NET CONFIG SERVER	Displays or modifies the configuration for the server service.
NET CONFIG WORKSTATION	Displays or modifies the configuration for the workstation.
NET CONTINUE	Activates suspended services.
NET FILE	Displays open shared files, including locks. Can also close files and remove locks.

NET GROUP	Displays and modifies global group information.
NET HELP	Help command for network commands.
NET HELPMSG	Displays information about a specific network error message.
NET LOCALGROUP	Displays and modifies local group information.
NET NAME	Displays, adds, or deletes messaging names for a workstation.
NET PAUSE	Suspends a service.
NET PRINT	Displays and controls print jobs.
NET SEND	Sends a message or file to other systems.
NET SESSION	Displays or disconnects a session between two systems.
NET SHARE	Creates, deletes, and displays shared resources on the system.
NET START	Starts a service or displays all running services. Enter the option on the command line to start the desired service.

Option	Service
ALERTER	Start the alerter.
COMPUTER	Computer browser.
DIRECTORY REPLICATOR	Directory replicator.
EVENTLOG	Eventlog.
LOCATOR	RPC locator.
MESSENGER	Messenger.
NBT	NetBIOS using TCP/IP.
NET LOGON	Net logon.
RPCSS	RPC subsystem.
SCHEDULE	Scheduler.
SERVER	Server.
UPS	UPS.
WORKSTATION	Workstation.

NET STATISTICS	Displays the statistics log.
NET STOP	Stops a service.
NET TIME	Displays or sets the time.
NET USE	Displays, connects, or disconnects a network service.
NET USER	Displays, adds, or modifies a user account.
NET VIEW	Displays servers on the network or resources shared by a particular server.

Configuration Commands

The commands in this table are used in the CONFIG.NT file located in the \WINNT\SYSTEM32 directory. Commands flagged as Not Used can be placed in the file for compatibility with applications but will be ignored by NT.

Command	Description
BUFFERS	Not used by NT.
CODEPAGE	OS/2 only.
COUNTRY	Sets the country information.
DEVICE	Loads a device driver.
DEVICEHIGH	Loads a device driver into upper memory.
DEVINFO	OS/2 only.
DOS	The DOS command specifies how the upper memory area will be used.
DRIVEPARM	OS/2 only.
ECHOCONFIG	ECHOCONFIG is used to display messages as CONFIG.NT is processed. It is similar to the ECHO DOS command.
FCBS	FCBS sets the number of file control blocks that can be opened simultaneously.
FILES	The FILES option sets the total number of files that can be opened simultaneously.
INSTALL	INSTALL loads a memory-resident program.
LASTDRIVE	Not used.

LIBPATH	OS/2 only.
PROTSHELL	OS/2 only.
SHELL	SHELL specifies which command interpreter is used and sets several options for the interpreter. Only CMD.EXE is supported.
STACKS	The STACKS option sets the amount of memory to be used for processing hardware interrupts.
SWITCHES	Not used.

DOS Subsystem Commands

The following table lists MS-DOS V5.0 commands that are supported for compatibility only. These are 16-bit commands that are supported directly by the command prompt subsystem.

Command	Description
APPEND	APPEND allows programs to open data files as if they were in the current directory. Similar to the PATH command, except it works for data files.
BACKUP	BACKUP copies files to a backup disk.
DEBUG	DEBUG is a testing tool for DOS programs.
EDIT	EDIT is the DOS V5.0 editor for text files.
EDLIN	EDLIN is a line-oriented text editor.
EXE2BIN	EXE2BIN converts executable (EXE) files to binary format.
GRAPHICS	GRAPHICS is a device driver that allows graphics files to print from the command prompt.
LOADFIX	LOADFIX loads a program at a fixed position in memory (above the first 64 KB) and then executes the program.
LOADHIGH (LH)	LH loads a program into the upper memory area.
MEM	MEM displays information on available memory and the amount of memory used by programs.
NLSFUNC	This command loads country information.
QBASIC	QBASIC is the Quick Basic program that ships with DOS V5.0.

SETVER	SETVER allows you to tie programs to certain versions of DOS. It is used for compatibility purposes when upgrading to a new version of DOS.
SHARE	This command starts file sharing and locking.

DOS V5. 0 Commands Not Supported by NT

Command	Description
ASSIGN	Not required.
CTTY	Not currently supported.
DOSSHELL	Not required because of the Windows interface.
EXPAND	Not required.
FASTOPEN	NT uses its own caching system.
FDISK	Disk Manager provides a superset of FDISK functionality.
JOIN	Not required.
MIRROR	Not supported.
SYS	Not supported.
UNDELETE	Not supported.
UNFORMAT	Not supported.

TCP/IP Commands

The next table covers utilities that are used for TCP/IP networks. TCP/IP must be installed to use these commands.

Command	Description
ARP	ARP displays and changes the IP-to-Ethernet translation tables.
FINGER	This command displays information about users on a remote system.
FTP	FTP transfers files to and from a remote system. The remote system must be running the FTP service. See TFTP.
HOSTNAME	This command prints the name of the current host.
NBTSTAT	NBTSTAT displays NetBIOS information.

NET START NBT	This command is used to start the NetBIOS service.
NET START SNMP	This command is used to start the SNMP service.
NET START TCPIP	This command is used to start the TCP/IP service.
NET START TELNET	This command is used to start the TELNET service.
NETSTAT	NETSTAT displays the contents of various network data structures.
PING	PING is a troubleshooting tool for echoing packets to a specified host.
RCP	RCP copies files between systems.
REXEC	This is a password-protected command that executes commands on a remote system. See RSH.
ROUTE	ROUTE is used to manually manipulate network routing tables.
RSH	This command executes commands on a remote system. See REXEC.
TELNET	TELNET is a terminal emulator for TCP/IP hosts.
TFTP	TFTP transfers files to and from another TCP/IP system. The other system must be running the FTP service. See FTP.

EXAMPLES OF NT COMMANDS

Opening a New Command Prompt Window

NT provides some very interesting options for command programs. The next example shows a command program named TESTST.BAT:

```
REM TESTST.BAT
START TEST3
DIR  D: > DIRD.TXT
```

TESTST.BAT is a simple program that illustrates some interesting options of the NT command prompt. The second line of the program uses the START command to execute the command TEST3.BAT. START starts another command prompt window and executes TEST3.BAT in the new window. While TEST3 is performing its tasks, the next line of our original command prompt executes: Instant multitasking using simple batch.commands!

TEST3.BAT is shown below:

```
@ECHO OFF
REM TEST3.BAT
TITLE "DIRECTORY OF E"
DIR E: > DIRE.TXT
EXIT
```

TEST3.BAT has two interesting commands. The TITLE command simply sets the text of the title bar for the command prompt executing the program. This is handy for letting users know what your program is doing and what each window is doing. The last line of the command file exits the command prompt window.

Connecting to Network Resources

LAN Manager users will feel right at home with the NET commands. Many of these commands are exactly the same as or only slightly modified from the LAN Manager versions.

The following command connects to a shared resource (ALR C on KENALR):

```
C:\USERS\DEFAULT\NET USE   I:   "\\KENALR\ALR C"
```

Note the quotation marks (") around the remote resource specification in the last example. NT requires quotation marks (") around a filename or share name whenever the name contains a space such as ALR C.

The NET command can also be used to list all connections to shared resources:

C:\USERS\DEFAULT\NET USE

```
Status              Local name      Remote name

OK                  G:              \\DELL320\C_DRIVE
OK                  I:              \\DELL320\C_DRIVE
The command completed successfully.
```

The NET VIEW command is used to display information about your network resources and systems. The default format of NET VIEW will list all servers in all domains or workgroups on your network:

C:\USERS\DEFAULT\NET *VIEW*

```
Server Name              Remark
\\DELL320
\\TRI-STAR               Ken's TriStar NT system
The command completed successfully.
```

The /DOMAIN:Domain_Name parameter can be used to show only computers on a specific domain. Domain_Name must be either a valid domain or a workgroup name.

NET VIEW can also be used to display information about a specific system. The format is the same as in our last example, except that a computer name is tagged onto the end:

C:\USERS\DEFAULT\NET *VIEW* *DELL320*

```
Shared resources at \\DELL320
Sharename          Type        Used as   Comment
C_DRIVE            Disk          G:
HPIII             Print
The command completed successfully.
```

Scheduling a Program

The AT command is used to schedule programs for execution at a later time or on a routine interval. AT uses the Scheduler service to actually schedule and execute the command. The Scheduler must be running on the local computer executing the AT command and on the remote system that will execute the command, if the command is going to run on a remote system.

The format of AT is fairly simple. The first format is used to delete a command that has already been scheduled:

```
AT [\\COMPUTERNAME] [[ID] [/DELETE [/YES]]
```

The next format is used to schedule a command:

```
AT [\\COMPUTERNAME] TIME [/EVERY:DATE | /NEXT:DATE]
      "COMMAND"
```

Entering AT with no parameters will display a list of all scheduled events for the local computer. Executing AT with a computer name will display scheduled events for that system. Executing AT with an ID number will display only information for that event.

The NT documentation adds a caution for systems using the AT command. Whenever the system date or time is changed on a system after you have scheduled a command on that system, you must synchronize the Scheduler by entering AT with no commands.

All scheduled event information is stored in the NT Registry. This preserves scheduled event information over reboots.

The next example executes a command every Friday at 1:40a.m.:

```
AT 1:40 /EVERY:F "TEST3"
```

AT also supports the redirection options of DOS to capture the output of a command. The next command illustrates how easy it is to capture the output of a command:

```
AT 00:00 "CLEANUP" > C:\UTILS\CLEANUP.LOG
```

You should always enclose the commands that AT will execute in quotation marks. The NT documentation requires the use of quotation marks in certain cases, but it is good habit to develop. There are situations in which AT will interpret AT options as part of the command unless you use quotation marks.

The next example removes all events from the Scheduler on the current system:

```
AT /DELETE
```

AT has a number of useful options for scheduling commands. Consult the NT command reference and the AT help information (AT /?) for more information.

Automating Tasks with Batch Programs

NT introduces the ability to run Windows programs from the command prompt. The next command will execute Word for Windows exactly like double-clicking on the Word for Windows icon in Program Manager:

```
C:\>WINWORD
```

This means that you can run Windows programs from within command (batch) files. You may be wondering what good it does it do to start an interactive program from a batch file. Most applications such as Word contain a powerful command language. The Word command language is called Word Basic and is one of the most powerful macro languages around. Let's talk about a real-world problem that could be solved using this technique.

There are many times that you need to run a batch report that collects data from a production system. Many times this report will be in an ASCII format that must be "prettied up" before it is sent to your manager. Let's say that our batch routine outputs an ASCII file from a production database and names the file WEEKLY.OUT. WEEKLY.OUT has all the numbers, including details and summary data. The only problem is the report looks very plain.

How do we "pretty up" this file without manual intervention? Word Basic to the rescue! Word has incredibly powerful formatting capabilities that can be tapped fairly easily. The macro should read the file WEEKLY.OUT, stuff the text into a word document, format the document, and print the file. This is a fairly simple macro that could combine the template capabilities of Word and the Word Basic language. Since this is not a Word book, I will refer you to the excellent book by Woody Leonhard, *Hacker's Guide to Word for Windows* (Addison-Wesley Publishing Co.).

The one trick we will use here is how to start a macro when Word starts. The trick is to place a /m and the macro name on the Word command line. The macro name should follow the /m with no spaces:

```
C:\> WINWORD /Mweekly_macro
```

Our complete NT command file may look like this:

```
@Echo Off
Weekly.EXE
WINWORD /Mweekly_macro
```

This simple command file starts only two programs: WEEKLY.EXE and WINWORD. The simplicity of the command may cause you to overlook the power of combining Windows programs and production programs in the same command file. NT allows you to use not only Windows programs but also third-party programs, producing some incredibly powerful combinations. For further thought, consider using the graphics engine in Microsoft Excel to format graphics straight off of a production database. The sky is really the limit for building integrated systems out of building blocks such as Word and Excel.

You can also crank up other Command Prompt windows for your applications from a command file. The START command will start a program in another window. This is very useful for command files that need to run another program and continue processing while the program runs.

The following program is a short batch file that will start three programs, each in its own window:

```
@echo off
echo This is an NT test of Start
start test1
start test2
start test3
```

The next program is a is the code used in TEST1, TEST2, and TEST3 in the last example. The TITLE command displays a new title in the title bar of the window. Exit closes the window:

```
TITLE "Directory of E"
DIR e: > dire.txt
EXIT
```

Hamilton C-Shell

The Hamilton C-shell is a layered product that brings the UNIX C-shell to NT. This product has been available for other operating systems for a number of years and was ported to NT in 1992. It has been running since Digital's Alpha AXP developer release.

The C-shell brings a lot of power to NT. Shell scripts (UNIX command files are called scripts) from any system that uses the C or Bourne shell can be easily moved to NT. This includes not only systems that run the Hamilton C-shell, but also most UNIX systems.

The C-shell is worth looking at by anyone who creates serious command files on NT, regardless of whether or not you have any UNIX scripts to bring over. The C-shell has a tremendously powerful set of commands that provide the capabilities for building powerful applications.

One of the more interesting command options is the ability to use the OpenVMS syntax of three periods (...) to traverse a directory structure. This means that a simple script routine can move throughout the directory tree, performing some task as it goes. Have you ever tried that with a DOS batch file?

CHAPTER 3

Windows NT Print Services

INTRODUCTION TO PRINTING ON NT

NT provides a number of features for managing printing on a standalone workstation or a network. The Print Manager application is the heart of the NT printing system, serving as a management tool for both local and network printers. Network users on other workstations running NT, Windows for Workgroups, LAN Manager, and other supported networks can also print to a printer attached to an NT workstation.

Users of a standalone system may not even be concerned with setting up or performing serious management chores for printers, because NT will install the printer during the NT installation procedure, if you select the printer attached to your workstation when requested by the Setup program. Users will also discover that Print Manager has the old familiar look and feel of the Windows V3.1 counterpart, except for several new options, such as a toolbar and new menu selections. Another change users will notice is how each print queue is now represented by its own window, instead of having one line for the queue, with the queue's documents listed underneath the queue. The main Print Manager screen is shown in the next illustration.

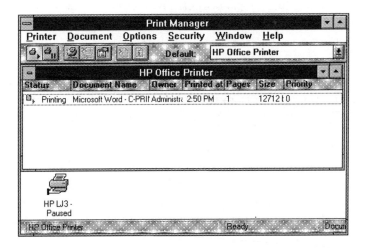

Print Manager

The Control Panel Printer applet we knew so well in Windows V3.1 now simply executes Print Manager.

How Does NT Handle Printers?

NT print services use the standard mechanism of spooling documents to print queues. A queue can be thought of as simply a list of documents (jobs) that are waiting to print. The order in which jobs print depends on each job's priority and other settings on the queue. The term *spooling* refers to an old acronym that originated in the mainframe and minicomputer days. Spool stands for Simultaneous Peripheral Operation Offline. Spooling simply means that some piece of software (Print Manger) will manage your printer while you continue to work, instead of making you wait until the document finished printing. You can bypass spooling by selecting the Print Directly to Selected Ports option on the Printer Details dialog.

An NT print queue can point to a physical printer on the local machine, or it may point to a network printer. Network printers use the same naming convention (UNC) that files do. For example, the print queue LASER on the workstation KEN would be specified as \\KEN\LASER. A print queue can also be directed to a file.

Printers on an NT system can be shared with other workstations on the network. Shared printers behave just like shared file resources. Users may connect, disconnect, and print to a shared printer using the standard tools of their operating system, such as Windows for Workgroups Print Manager, Windows V3.1 Control Panel Printers applet, and LAN Manager Net Use. After a user has connected to a printer, the printer behaves just like a local printer. The user may not even be aware that the printer is not locally attached if he or she did not have to walk to the printer to obtain the output.

The next figure shows how a printer is fed from a print queue. This example uses two queues that point to the same printer. Notice that both queues are connected to the same printer. The connection from the queues to the printer is purely symbolic, because it is actually done in software by the NT printing system.

Multiple Queues Can Point to the Same Printer

NT allows multiple print queues to point to the same physical printer. This is useful when you wish to segregate jobs by user or when different users do not have the same access characteristics. For instance, you might want to restrict network users' access to the printer while allowing local users complete access.

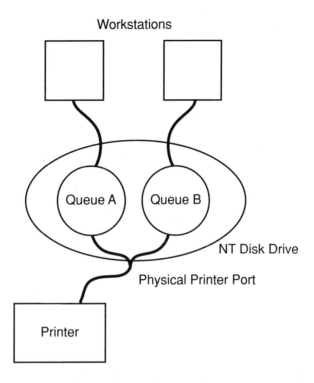

NT Print Queues

The figure above shows two print queues that feed the same printer. Queue A is open to all users but has a limited time of operation and a lower default priority. Queue B is limited to the main user of the workstation and has a high priority and no restrictions. A printer serviced by these two queues will always print the main user's documents first and will restrict network users to only certain hours of the day.

Queues Can Service Multiple Printers

NT can print to multiple printers from one queue. This is useful when you have a large volume of printing that will take a long time to print on the normal printer or may cause a backlog on one printer.

When multiple printers are serviced by one queue, the printers are treated as a printer pool. NT will automatically balance printing over the printers in the pool. Using multiple printers also provides some fault tolerance, because if one printer fails, the other printers will keep on printing. For more information about this subject, see the Additional Printer Details Dialog section of this chapter.

The capability to split a print queue over multiple ports is particularly useful in an area where you have lots of users printing to a print queue. You can point the queue to two or more similar printers and achieve the throughput of a high-speed network printer. This could be a permanent solution, or a temporary solution when you have to pump out a tremendous amount of paper for a mailing or large presentation.

Using Print Manager

Print Manager controls and manages printers for NT systems. The layout of the screen is similar to that of the Windows V3.1 Print Manager, except for the toolbar and the use of separate windows for each printer. The NT Print Manager has many more features than the V3.1 Print Manager, especially in the area of networks and printer management. NT's Print Manager also has security features for controlling who can access a printer and what actions they can perform, when the printer can be accessed, and the priority of documents waiting to print.

Print Manager displays the status of both local printers and network printers. This includes whether the printer is active, paused, or stalled. The status of each document waiting to print is also displayed. The next figure illustrates the main Print Manager window.

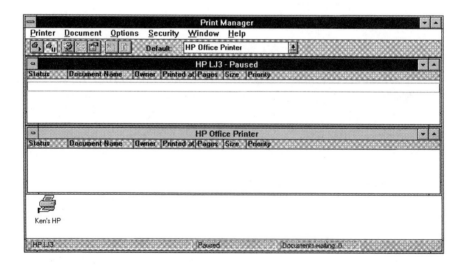

Print Manager

The columns in a Printer window can be resized in the same manner as a spreadsheet column. Move the mouse over the separator line between the column headers until the pointer turns into a double arrow, then press the left button and drag the column to the desired width.

Print Manager uses a toolbar similar to the one in File Manager to provide quick access to a number of functions. These include connecting to network printers, pausing and resuming a printer or document, accessing printer and document details, and changing the default printer.

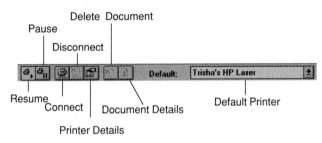

Print Manager Toolbar

The toolbar buttons are simply shortcuts to certain menu commands. All menu commands are not listed on the toolbar.

You can also change the default printer by choosing a new printer from the drop-down list. The default printer is the one used by Windows applications unless you choose a specific printer within the application.

You can select a document by clicking the document name with the left mouse button. Clicking the right mouse button on a selected document will deselect the document.

Print Manager also displays some information when a Printers window is minimized. The next figure displays the icons for two different printers.

Print Manager Icons for Multiple Printers

Notice the share indicator on Ken's HP LJIII, showing that the printer is shared. This gives you a quick look at your printers and their status. If a printer is paused, the printer name will contain "- Paused" at the end of the name.

Let's cover several functions Print Manager performs and see how they relate to things we have already learned about NT.

Adding Print Queues

Print queues can be added by selecting Create Printer from the Printer menu in Print Manager. Print Manager will display the Printer Properties dialog, which provides controls for installing a new printer driver.

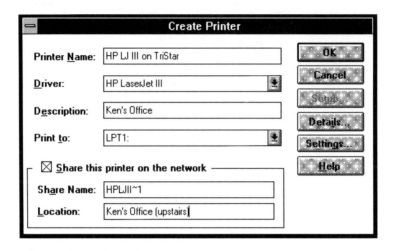

Printer Properties Dialog for Installing a Printer

Once the dialog has been displayed, the installation process can be completed by completing the following steps:

1. Enter the printer's name.

2. Select the printer driver from the drop-down list. If this driver is not already installed on your system, you will need the NT distribution media (diskettes, CD-ROM, or network drive), or the printer driver media if this is not a standard NT printer driver.

3. Enter a description for the printer (optional).

4. Select the port to which the printer will be attached.

5. Enter the Share information if the printer will be a shared printer.

6. Select optional parameters for the printer (Details, Settings, Permissions).

7. Click OK.

8. Next, Print Manager will display the Setup dialog for the printer. Select options on this dialog and click OK.

Removing a Print Queue

A print queue can be removed by selecting the Printer/Remove Printer menu option. Selecting Remove Printer will delete the currently selected printer. A confirmation box with the name of the printer will be displayed to make sure you want to remove the printer.

Stopping and Restarting a Printer or Document

The Pause and Resume functions are both available on the Print menu as well as the toolbar.

Resume will restart a printer or document that has been paused for some reason. A printer may be paused because it ran out of paper, has a paper jam, or was explicitly paused by a user. The printer can be restarted by selecting it in the Print Manager window and clicking on Resume. The printer will restart and the status will change to blank as long as the reason the printer was stopped has been corrected.

Resume will also work on a document if a document is selected instead of a printer. You can click on a document and then click Resume to restart the document.

Pause performs exactly the opposite function of Resume. Selecting a printer or document and then clicking Pause will stop the printer or document. Pause is a handy tool to use when you want to temporarily hold a document in queue while others print. Pause is also useful when you need to stop a printer for a short time to change paper or perform some other task.

Connecting to a Shared Network Printer

The Connect to Printer function is available on the toolbar and the Printer menu. It displays the standard Connect dialog, similar to the one in File Manager. Selecting a Workgroup or domain will list all the shared printers in the Workgroup or domain. Select the desired printer by double-clicking the printer name or clicking the name and clicking OK.

The Connect to Printer dialog displays several bits of useful information about the network printers. Notice the Printer Information box at the bottom of the dialog. This box will display the driver, status, and number of documents waiting for the selected printer. This is very helpful, because many times you need to print something in a hurry and want to find an available printer. Clicking on a workgroup or domain will display all the available printers. Simply click on a printer or use the arrow key to move down the list until you find a printer with the correct driver (for example, HP LaserJet III), the status of Ready, and the fewest number of documents waiting.

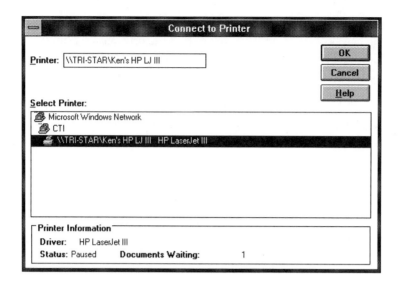

Connect to Printer Dialog

NT will automatically reconnect to shared printer resources when it reboots.

Removing a Printer Connection

The Remove Printer function is available on the Printer menu and the toolbar.

You may want to remove a printer connection when you no longer require the use of the printer or possibly if there is a problem with the printer. To remove a printer, click on the Remove Printer Connection button, which will display the Remove Connection dialog. Select the printer connection to remove and click OK or double-click the connection.

The Remove button is also available on the Print menu.

Changing Printer Properties

The Printer Properties button is available on the toolbar and the Printer menu.

The Printer Properties dialog is shown in the next figure. This dialog contains the setup parameters for the selected printer. The dialog provides a handy place to quickly change printer parameters. You should also notice that the Share this Printer on the Network Box and Share Name at the bottom of the dialog allow you to share the printer by clicking on the Share box and filling in the Share name. You can accomplish several tasks at once with this dialog because it centralizes so many functions in one place. The option buttons on the right also provide access to other parameters via separate dialogs.

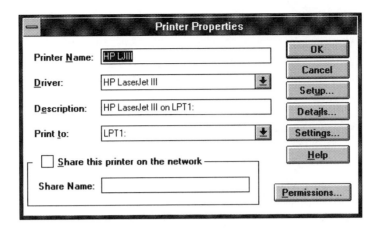

Printer Properties Dialog

The following table describes the fields of the dialog.

Option	Description
Printer Name	Printer Name is the name of the printer and is the default Share name. This name is also used by application program dialogs referencing printers.
Driver	The Driver field is a drop-down list that contains the name of the printer driver for this printer. Printer drivers are supplied with NT and are also available from printer manufacturers and other vendors. Drivers and updates are also available from CompuServe and the Microsoft download service.
	You can also change a driver by clicking the arrow beside the list and selecting a new driver.
Description	This field can be used to add an additional description for the printer.
Print To	The Print To field specifies which port the physical printer is connected to.
	You can change the port by clicking a new port. The Details button also allows you to select additional ports if you have multiple printers for a queue.
	Choosing the Other option from the list will display a dialog to connect the printer to a network device or an unlisted port.

Share this Printer on the Network	This check box will turn on the Share Name field network when clicked and will automatically share the printer.
Share Name	The Share name is the name you wish to use for sharing the printer over the network. The default Share names is the same as the Printer name.

Additional Printer Details Dialog

The Details button on the main Printer Properties dialog displays the following dialog, which controls several aspects of a printer. Be very careful with the options on this dialog, because it can stop your printer from functioning. This includes all fields except for the location field, which is simply a reference to the physical location of the printer.

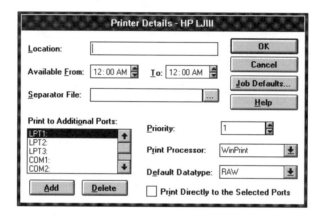

Printer Details Dialog

The Printer Details dialog contains a number of options that control how a printer functions. This is a very useful dialog for changing the characteristics of the operation of the printer. Some options, such as Print to Additional Ports, Print Processor, Default Datatype, and Print Directly to the Selected Ports, should not be touched once the printer is up and running. Others, such as Available From, Separator File, and Priority, may be changed from time to time to modify the use characteristics of the printer. The following table describes each option.

Option	Description
Location	This is a text field defining the location (for example, Ken's office) of the printer. It serves as a reference only.
Available From/ To	This field specifies when the printer is available to print documents. The printer will accept documents at any time but will print only between the From and To hours.
Separator File	A separator file can be used to separate printed documents as they are printed. The separator file places a sheet of paper between each document and determines what is printed on the separator page. Click on the ... button to display a list of separator files.
Print to Additional Ports	This option selects additional ports for the selected print queue. Documents will be automatically printed on printers connected to the additional ports. To select a local port, click the arrow beside the list and select a port.
Priority	Sets the priority of the printer (1-99).
Print Processor	This selects the processor to use for this printer. A print processor is a program that manages the printer.
Default Datatype	This field should not be changed except in rare instances and then only by experienced users.
Print Directly to the Selected Ports	Selecting this check box will bypass print spooling. This will cause the printer to print slightly faster but will degrade the performance of your system.

Print Job Default Characteristics

The Job Defaults button from Printer Details displays the Document Properties dialog. Settings that are changed when accessing this dialog through Job Defaults will be used as the defaults for all documents for the printer. Any items that are set by the application that created the print job will override the defaults.

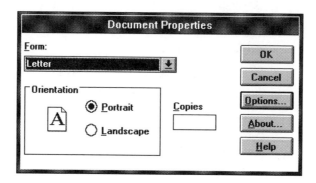

Document Properties Dialog

Print Settings

The Configure Port dialog is displayed by clicking the Settings button on Printer Details. The Configure Port dialog is used to configure the port parameters for a communications port (LPT or COM). The default settings in this dialog are usually sufficient. The dialog will vary depending on what type of port you have selected, either Parallel or Serial.

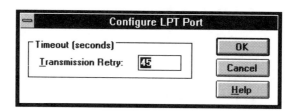

Configure LPT Port Dialog

Queue and Print Job Parameters

Each document listed in Print Manager has certain characteristics that determine how it will print. The following dialog shows the different parameters that control how a document prints. Notice the variety of information that is contained in this dialog. Information is available concerning the title of the document (usually including the application that created it), its size, where and when it was printed, the document's owner, and the document's priority. A time range can also be specified for a document, showing the time it can start printing and the latest time it can print.

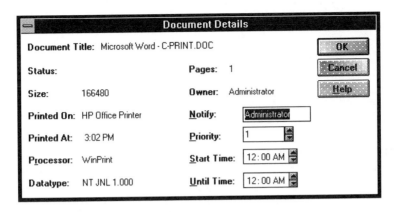

Print Manager Document Details Dialog

Two of the most frequently used boxes in this dialog are the Priority and Notify options. Raising a document's priority will cause the document to print before documents with lower priorities. Priorities can range from 1 (lowest) to 99 (highest).

Placing a username in the Notify box will cause NT to notify that user when the document completes printing. This is useful when you are printing a long document on a remote printer and there are lots of other documents in the queue.

Selecting a document and clicking on Document Details will display the Document Properties dialog. This dialog provides a handy way to change several print options before a document actually starts printing. You must react fairly quickly to access this dialog, or your job may already be printing, unless of course the printer is paused or there are lots of other documents ahead of the one you want. The safest way to access this dialog is to pause the document you wish to change as soon as you realize that it should be changed, then click on Document Details.

The quickest way to access a Documents Details dialog is by double-clicking the document. The dialog can also be accessed by selecting Details from the Document menu or clicking on the Document Details button on the toolbar.

Options in the left column (Document Title, Status, and so on), Pages, and Owner are for reference only and cannot be changed.

You can change the following parameters for documents that you have sent to the printer:

◆ Who will be notified when the document has been printed.

◆ The range of time in which the document can be printed.

◆ The document's priority.

◆ The document's print processor.

You must have administrative permission to change parameters for documents that other users have printed.

Changing Printer Driver Properties

The Setup function will display another Printer Properties dialog with additional properties. Setup can be accessed from the Printer Properties dialog. The following figure shows a sample of a dialog for a Hewlett-Packard LaserJet. This example is the Setup dialog from Windows V3.1.

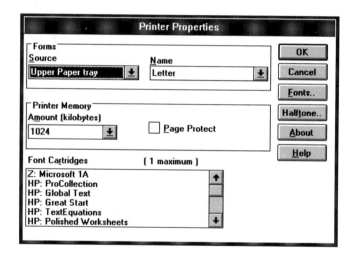

Additional Printer Properties Dialog

The top area of the dialog is boxed off with a label of Forms and contains two fields: Source and Name. The Source field determines where the paper for the printer will feed from. For laser printers this is usually Upper Paper Tray, Lower Paper Tray, or Manual Feed.

The exact items in this dialog and the dialogs called from this dialog are determined by your printer driver and will vary from printer to printer. You should review the documentation for your printer driver and consult the help files for the driver to determine the specific features the driver offers.

The options on this dialog and others dialogs that may be accessible from here should be changed with care, because they can affect the operating characteristics of the printer.

Deleting a Document from a Queue

Deleting a document from a queue is a simple task. Select a document and click the Delete Document button, and the document vanishes from the queue. You can also delete a document by selecting the document and pressing the Delete key on the keyboard. You will receive a warning message and a chance to cancel the operation if the document is already printing.

The Delete option should be used with caution on shared printers. Users with Manage Documents or Full Control permission for a printer can easily blow away the documents of other users.

The Printer/Purge Printer menu option will delete all documents for a printer. Selecting this option will trigger a confirmation dialog just to make sure you really want to delete all documents.

Using Printer Forms

Printers that are used in a network environment sooner or later begin to suffer the "What forms in the printer?" problem. This is especially a problem on printers that can use many different types of forms such as those listed below.

Form Type	Description
Invoice	Invoices are a type of business form that are usually multi-part preprinted forms. These forms usually run on a dot-matrix printer but may also be printed on a laser printer if single-part forms are used.
Letterhead	Letterhead is typically a high-quality bond paper that is pre-printed with a company logo and address.
Plain	Plain paper refers to plain white laser printer paper or plain (or green-bar) dot-matrix paper.
Envelopes	Envelopes can vary in size and are available in many different types and weights.

The problem of managing forms on a network printer is very tricky. How does a user know what form is currently on the printer? How does he know the form will still be mounted when his print job starts to print? How does the person in charge of the printer know when she can safely change from one paper type to another? The answer is in forms control.

The concept of printer forms has been around for many years and was pioneered on minicomputers and mainframes. Printer forms work by tagging a form name and print characteristics to a form definition. For instance, in the Forms dialog, the name Letter identifies a form that has a certain size (8 1/2 x 11), specific margins, and a Units identifier (Metric or English). NT also provides a field for a one-line form description.

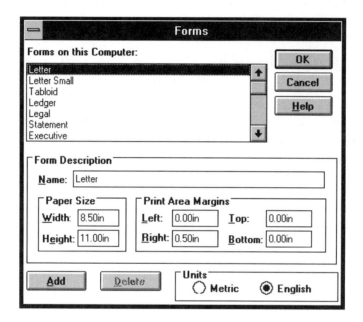

Forms Dialog

Users can add custom forms to the forms definitions. Notice that the Delete button works only with user-created forms. It is grayed out when a standard NT form is selected.

Managing Remote Printers

The Server Viewer options allows you to view printer information from other compatible systems. This option works just like the connect dialog:

1. Select a workgroup.

2. Select a computer to view.

3. Click OK.

You can also select a computer to view by typing the name in the Computer field. Click OK after you have entered the name.

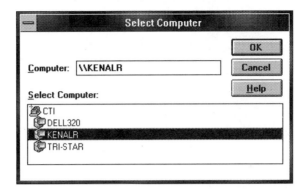

Select Computer Dialog

After you have selected the computer to view, NT will display that computer with its printers. You can minimize a printer's window, and it will appear as an icon in the bottom of the Print Manager window.

Having remote access to the parameters of NT network printers is an extremely powerful tool. This capability means that you can change parameters such as time available or priority on remote printers. You could also use the remote management feature to pause and restart queues or to change advanced options.

Are you beginning to get the feeling that you can manage NT resources from many different machines by sitting at your desk? Right! Most management applications in the base NT package allow you to monitor or change resources from different systems on the network. The systems you can monitor and manage in this manner are not limited to NT systems; they simply must be NT-compatible. I suspect this means that Windows for Workgroups and other systems will begin to add features that allow them to talk to NT workstations. A number of management programs are now or will soon be available that also provide management tools for NT systems.

Options Menu
The Options menu contains three selections. Each selection has an on or off setting indicated by a check mark.

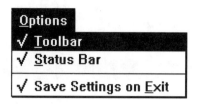

Options Menu

The first two selections control the display of the Toolbar and Status Bar. Clicking on either selection will toggle the display on or off.

The familiar Save Settings on Exit command is also on this menu.

CHAPTER 4

Windows NT Networking

NETWORK ARCHITECTURE

Introduction to NT Networking

Local- and wide-area networks have become much more interesting with the introduction of NT and the latest releases of Windows V3.x. Networks can be created for sharing disk and print services by connecting several workstations together and using Windows for Workgroups, the Workgroup Connection, and/or NT. This simple network will not have sophisticated user-level security or sophisticated server controls, but it will work very nicely for a small office or other group of users who need to share only some files and printers. A small NT or combination NT, Windows for Workgroups, and the Workgroup Connection LAN is an ideal system, because many businesses are overwhelmed by a NetWare LAN and do not require high-level security; many of these users share passwords anyway.

More-complex LANs can use the features of a full-blown network such as Pathworks, NetWare, or Windows NT Advanced Server. These networks offer far more features for security, file sharing, electronic mail, and network management. NT's support for these networks allows it to fully participate in existing networks based on most popular technologies. This support for other networks also provides an easy migration path for users who wish to move from one technology or the other to a total NT-based system.

NT Desktop

NT will support simple networks by itself with no other LAN software. Any NT or Windows for Workgroups workstation on the LAN can participate as a node in the network, using and offering services from and to other nodes. The Windows NT base package provides support for networks of two to fifty nodes but does not physically limit the number of network nodes or users.

Out-of-the-box network functionally is available by installing NT, Microsoft Workgroup Connection, or Windows for Workgroups on multiple machines with network connections and configuring NT to recognize the network. This process is very simple and is no more complicated than installing a Windows for Workgroups network.

The NT base package does not include server-level fault tolerance and other management features for large networks. Most large network installations will probably decide to use the NT Advanced Server or will use NT in conjunction with another network such as NetWare or Pathworks. NT provides a very open architecture for other network vendors. We will see an example of this when we look at the Pathworks products later in this chapter.

Windows NT Advanced Server

The Windows NT Advanced Server product provides NT workstations with the ability to fully participate in a LAN Manager-based network, as either a client or server. Windows NT Advanced Server has all the features normally expected on LAN Manager, including domains, user- and share-level security, and easy-to-use management tools. The broad range of hardware supported by NT is a valuable asset for LAN Manager-based servers because of the tremendous horsepower available for different sizes of systems.

Windows NT Advanced Server brings powerful network features to NT. Support for domains, true fault tolerance, and user-level security are just a few of the features that make LAN Manager a powerful option for a network server.

Windows NT Advanced Server also has features that will make managing large networks a much simpler task. Features are also provided for very large networks with large numbers of workstations and servers.

It is critical that everyone understand that Windows NT Advanced Server is not required for your NT network. For most networks that have simple file or printer sharing requirements, plain NT will work just fine. This is especially true if your network has fewer than twenty client workstations. You may not even need Windows NT Advanced Server for larger networks unless your file resources grow very large or you have a requirement for other NT features. The best approach for a small network is to start with a simple NT server and work your way up. Upgrading to Windows NT Advanced Server will be a simple task if your needs require it later on.

Other Networks

Other networks for NT will be discussed at other points of this chapter and in Chapter 5. NT is designed to support not only LAN Manager networks but also almost any other network that currently exists or may come out in the future. The layered architecture of NT allows a network to plug into the NT architecture easily. Pathworks for Windows NT is an example of a network that was quickly and efficiently ported to NT. As NT matures, I am sure that it will become even more network aware and support an ever-widening range of networks and network management tools.

BUILDING A SMALL NT NETWORK

Typical users of a base NT network will be small businesses or departments and other small groups of people that need to connect several machines running NT, DOS V6.0, or Windows for Workgroups. The base networking capability of NT provides tremendous value for these users because of the native support for sharing files and printers without adding another layer of network software.

Many people have failed to appreciate how NT can revolutionize the network for many organizations, especially small to medium-size companies with networks of five to fifty or more workstations. NT provides the tools to build this size network very quickly. Traditional networks of this size have been based on Novell's NetWare or some other vendor's system. These networks often required server licenses that cost $2,000 to $5,000 per server. The total cost for such a server often runs between $9,000 to $15,000, including hardware and software. I have seen NetWare servers that cost more than $35,000.

NT and Windows for Workgroups change the landscape for these smaller networks. At less than $500, the cost of NT software is very small compared to a typical network server. Workstations on the network only require Windows for Workgroups to participate in the network.

A small network can be set up very quickly with an NT server and Windows for Workgroups clients. The NT server can be configured almost identical to a normal NetWare or LAN Manager server by maintaining user accounts on one NT machine that is used exclusively as a file server. One or two large disk drives, a tape drive and lots of memory will quickly turn an NT workstation into a suitable server.

NT also adds some server features that some other networks do not, namely the ability to have a tape drive on the server itself, to have a friendly interface on the server, and to run batch or interactive applications on the server.

The following figure illustrates a simple network with Windows for Workgroups clients.

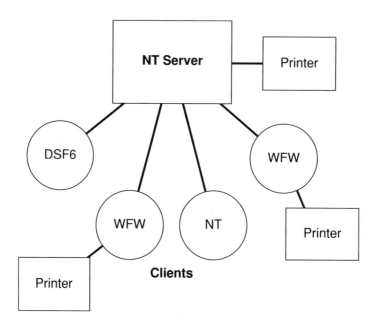

NT Server-Based Network

This network uses any NT machine for the server on a small network. No extra network software is required for the network, because Windows for Workgroups and NT can access the shared resources on the NT server. Each machine can also access shared resources on the Windows for Workgroups and other NT machines. Notice the printers that are attached to the Windows for Workgroups clients and the NT server. The printer-sharing facilities of Windows for Workgroups and NT provide the facilities for sharing printers with the other workstations without using print servers or other special software or hardware. This type of network not only reduces the cost of the network, but it also makes managing many of the network's resources easier because of the resource management features of both NT and Windows for Workgroups.

The steps to create this cost-effective network are simple:

1. Install the network hardware in each machine.

2. Write down the hardware configuration for each card. (I usually leave the configuration at the defaults unless there is special hardware in the PC.)

3. Install NT on the server.

4. Install the network software on each client if it is not already installed. Windows for Workgroups and NT clients do not require any additional software.

5. Configure the server and each client for the network.

6. Reboot the server and each client.

7. Share files and printers on the server.

8. Add remote-access accounts for each user who will access resources on the server.

9. Connect to the shared services from each client workstation.

These steps may sound trivial to a novice or to someone who has struggled through an installation of NetWare or some other big-time network, but they work. NT will usually recognize the network adapter and its settings upon installation in your system. It is simple to enter the values (if you perform Step 2) if NT does not recognize your adapter. Each step to building your network will be covered in detail later in this chapter, but first let's look at an overview of NT's networking capabilities and some layered network products that can be added to NT.

Network Protocols

A network protocol is a set of rules that specify how to communicate over a network. Computer systems must use the same protocol when they communicate with each other. For instance, a system using DECnet cannot communicate with one using TCP/IP. NT supports a number of protocols, including those supported by the most popular networks. Examples of network protocols supported by NT are TCP/IP, NetBEUI, IPX, and DECnet. NT also supports multiple protocols at the same time, allowing your system to communicate with different systems that are not using the same protocol.

NT's native protocol for communicating with other NT systems is NetBEUI. NetBEUI is used by NT and many other networks, including Windows for Workgroups. Because NetBEUI is supported by all Microsoft networks, the networks can work together right out of the box.

NT provides support for TCP/IP, allowing NT to participate in networks that use TCP/IP after the TCP/IP driver is loaded and started. NT can share information and resources with these systems. The other protocols are used by other systems in the same manner as TCP/IP. TCP/IP is the native protocol for almost every UNIX system and is quickly gaining a large market share for other systems, as well.

Most Digital systems use DECnet for communicating over a network, although they can also support TCP/IP. The following table lists the standard protocols supported by NT.

Protocol	Shipped w/NT	Description
NetBEUI	Yes	The NetBEUI protocol is the second generation of NetBIOS. The native NT protocol is the native Microsoft NetBEUI protocol.
IPX	No	IPX is the native NetWare protocol. IPX is used for connecting to Net Ware servers. The IPX protocol is supported by the NetWare for NT client software from Novell. The NetWare client can be obtained direct from Novell or from CompuServe.
TCP/IP	Yes	The TCP/IP protocol is supported on all UNIX platforms and many other systems.
DECnet	No	DECnet is Digital's network protocol. NT supports DECnet via the Pathworks for Windows NT layered product from Digital.

NT can use two or more protocols simultaneously. A typical network may have NT clients and servers, NetWare or Pathworks clients and servers, and possibly some UNIX clients and servers. In this type of network, NT may be using NetBEUI to communicate with the other NT systems, TCP/IP for the UNIX systems, DECnet for Pathworks, and IPX for NetWare. Because NT is not constrained by the memory barriers of DOS, loading multiple network protocols at the same time does not affect the capabilities of an NT system.

HOW DO I SET UP MY NT NETWORK?

Setting up your NT network begins with installing NT. During the installation process, NT will try to figure out what type of network adapter you have in your machine. You may need to help NT during the installation process by specifying which card you are using or at least verifying that NT has chosen the correct card. You may also need to specify the parameters for the card and your network. This information includes things such as the workgroup or domain name for the machine and the Interrupt Request (IRQ) and memory settings for your network card. Each of these items is discussed later in this section.

The primary emphasis of this section is on networking the base NT product. The server version of NT builds on the basic functionality of the base product, and it would require a book twice this size to review both products.

Installing a Network Card

The first step in installing a network card in your system is gathering some information about your system. This information will mostly concern your network adapter card and your network. It is a good idea to document this information for each machine on your network and to store the documents in a safe place for later reference. Be sure to identify each machine with a unique name; you will need this for NT anyway.

The first step in our documentation process is to gather some information about your network card and system. First determine what hardware services are currently used in your system. This is important, because installing two hardware devices that use the same hardware service will cause major problems with your system. The next sections in this chapter cover possible conflicts. Many of these items may not apply to some systems running NT because of differences in the design of the hardware. Some newer network cards are software configurable via an installation program that ships with the adapter. If you are using an older network card that requires you to manually set configuration parameters, you must be very careful to correctly set the switches and jumpers before installing the card.

The specific items you should record are card manufacturer, model number, IRQ address, base, memory address, and any other settings on the card.

Second, find out the name of your workgroup or domain. If the workstation you are installing is on a new network, you must determine the workgroup and domain name. Once you have this information, write it down in your network document.

Third, determine the computer name for the workstation you are installing. Write the computer name on the same page as the adapter information for the workstation. Once you have collected this information, you are ready to install your network adapter and software.

Interrupts

An IRQ is a physical line to the CPU that is used by a device to interrupt the CPU when a device needs control of the CPU or is ready to receive or pass information from or to the CPU. PCs have a limited number of interrupts available for devices, because many IRQs are already used by standard devices, such as a hard disk, floppy, parallel interface or port, making the number of available interrupts very small. The problem is compounded when you add many special devices such as sound cards or CD-ROM drives to your PC, because most of them require their own IRQ. The following chart illustrates the normal assignments for IRQs on a typical PC. This may vary from one PC to another, so be sure to check out your system manuals. The list of IRQs in the chart is the same for both a DELL 486/33 and an ALR Ranger 486/25 laptop.

IRQ	Description
0	Timer Clock
1	Keyboard
2	Second 8259A
3	Com2: Com4:
4	Com1: Com3
5	LPT2
6	Floppy Disk
7	LPT1:
8	Redirected IRQ2
9 - 12	Reserved
13	Math Coprocessor
14	Fixed Disk
15	Reserved (sometimes this one is OK to use)

Most network cards shipping today are preset to use certain IRQs and other defaults. These defaults will work fine in most systems unless you have a lot of other devices that are using the same interrupts or other settings. SCSI adapters are prone to causing interrupt conflicts with network adapters. The defaults used by most adapter manufacturers are IRQ = 2, 5, or 10; I/O base port = 02E; and base memory address = D000. The I/O base port and the base memory addresses are both in hex.

IRQ conflicts are a possible source of problems with your system. IRQ conflicts will usually result in NT's complaining about not finding the network adapter. If you experience problems that may be related to an IRQ, try switching to a new IRQ. Interrupts 2, 3, 5, and 9 are usually good choices.

Memory Base Address

A network card will normally map its memory into a section of the PC's memory between 640 KB and 1 MB. A typical default address is D000. The memory occupied by the adapter will usually be from 32 to 64 KB in size. Some network cards such as the EtherLinkIII from 3Com Corp. do not map into the PC's memory. A new Ethernet card from Digital uses only 2 KB of memory.

Network Adapters

There are many types of network cards, including cards of different ages. Network technology has expanded greatly during the past 10 years, providing us with many advancements in technology and leaving us with network cards of varying levels of sophistication. For instance, the 3Com EtherlinkII card has jumpers and switches for setting its configuration. You must determine each setting for the EtherLinkII manu-ally and set the switches and jumpers before installing the card. The newer EtherLinkIII has no switches or jumpers and is set by using a software program. The EtherLinkIII software will even try to figure out which settings it should use in order to minimize conflicts with your system.

Some newer PCs further simplify or complicate the issue by having factory-installed network capabilities. Many of these newer PCs will also come with NT and possibly a network card preinstalled, in which case you may not have to bother with installing the network card or configuring the network software except for workgroup and computer name.

The next step to installing your network adapter is to shut down the machine and prepare it for the installation of the card. You should carefully follow the steps in the network card's documentation and your documentation throughout this process, because different machines and network cards may not have the same installation procedures. Make sure the machine is turned off and unplugged from its power source. Handle the network card and other devices in the PC with care and do not touch the components on the boards or the card edge connectors. Make sure the network adapter is seated fully in the machine and secure the card with a screw or other device per your machine's instructions.

Installing the Network Driver Software

After the network adapter is installed in the machine, you are ready to configure the hardware. You can skip this step if you install NT after the network card is installed, because you will complete this process during the installation.

The Networks applet in Control Panel is used to complete the installation of the network software. Clicking the Add Adapter button will bring up the following dialog.

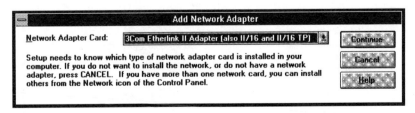

Network Adapter Setup Dialog

This dialog allows you to select your network driver from the list box. If your network adapter is not listed, choose the Other or not listed option. You will be prompted for the location of the driver files, either the NT installation disks or the driver disk that was shipped with your network adapter. At the prompt, insert the disk and follow the prompts to complete the operation. During the installation, the driver files will be copied to the \WINNT\SYSTEM32\DRIVERS directory.

Changing Network Hardware Settings

The Configure icon will allow you to change the settings for your network adapter. This includes the type of adapter and its settings, such as the IRQ and memory address.

NT can support multiple network adapters in a single PC. Each adapter can support a different network topology, such as Ethernet or Token Ring, or all the drivers may support the same topology. When other adapters are used, they will be listed in the Network Adapters box of the Network dialog. An example of multiple adapters is a PC that uses an Ethernet adapter to connect to a Windows for Workgroups network and a Token Ring adapter to connect to a NetWare network. A single adapter may be used for both systems, but the flexibility of using multiple adapters is very handy for connecting to two or more networks that use different network topologies — Ethernet and Token Ring, for example. You may improve the throughput of your NT system by using multiple adapters for the same topology and splitting your network into segments.

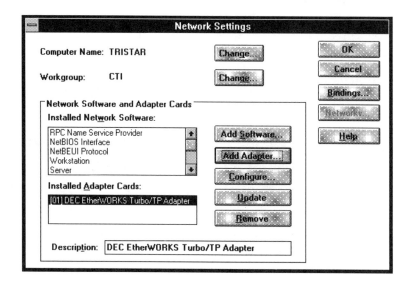

Network Settings Dialog

The Network Settings dialog provides a list of the currently installed network adapters in the system. The buttons should be self-explanatory, except for the Configure button. Configure brings up the following dialog box for changing the settings of the adapter.

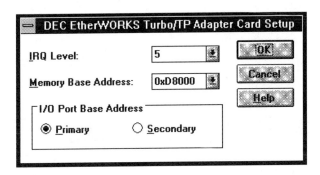

Network Configuration Dialog

The options in this dialog box will vary from one adapter to another, because the network driver controls the options required for that particular adapter. This flexibility allows NT to take advantage of new hardware by installing an updated driver from the adapter vendor. Note that the address shown in the above example (0xD8000) is the normal default address for some SCSI adapters.

The options listed in the box above are for a Digital Etherworks adapter.

Option	Description
IRQ Level	The interrupt value for your adapter. See the Interrupts section of this chapter.
Memory Base Address	Starting memory address for the adapter. See the Base Memory Address section of this chapter.
I/O Port Base Address	The I/O port base address.

After you have made changes to the network adapter settings, the system must be restarted for the settings to take effect. Click Yes on the Restart Computer dialog when NT prompts you to restart the system.

Adding or Modifying Protocols

The Control Panel Networks applet is used to install or change the configuration of network software and protocols. The process is very simple: Click on the Install Software button and select the desired software or protocol from the list. NT provides the Other category for protocols that are supplied from other vendors and are not listed. After you have selected your software and protocol follow the instructions to complete the task.

The Configure button is used to access the configuration parameters of a particular protocol. This button activates the Configure software dialog when you have selected a Software driver from the list box. It is the same button that configures the adapter when you have selected an adapter in the list box. Not all software drivers can be configured, and selecting one of these will generate an error dialog.

The following figure shows a typical setup dialog for a software driver. This particular dialog is for the NetBEUI protocol.

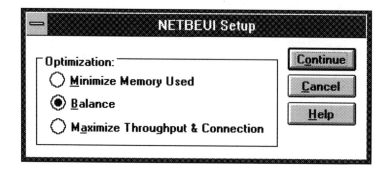

NetBEUI Protocol Setup Dialog

Exercise care in selecting protocols and other network settings when other networks are used with NT. You may lose functionality by using another network driver instead of the NT driver for a particular network.

Workgroup and Computer Names

After the network adapter is installed and configured, you may also need to enter the Workgroup name of your network and the computer name for your system. Both of these names can be up to fifteen characters long. The computer name is required for all NT systems, while the workgroup name is required only if your system will be part of a workgroup. The Network applet is used to enter or change both names. All NT machines in a Workgroup must have the same Workgroup name, and each machine must have a different computer name.

The Domain button brings up the following dialog. Click on Workgroup Name and enter your workgroup name in the box. If your network is part of a LAN Manager domain, you should select Domain Name and enter the name for the LAN Manger domain. If you are using NT in a LAN Manager network, check with the network administrator to obtain the required domain name and password.

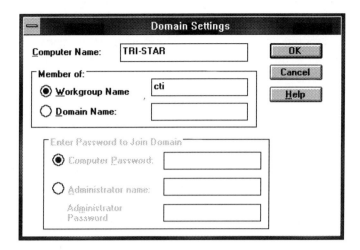

Domain Settings Dialog

The computer name for your system is also shown in this dialog. The computer name is used to identify the system on the network and must be unique within the network. This is the name that will show up in the browse dialog box when other systems are connecting to this systems shared resources. It is the same name that is used in the UNC naming conventions to connect to these resources.

MANAGEMENT

NT provides a number of tools for managing your network. These include the Performance Monitor, Event Viewer, Control Panel, Print Manager, File Manager, and the NET command line program.

NT is a friendly network workstation or server operating system because it automatically monitors its operation and adjusts its configuration to maintain optimum performance. Automatic optimization will only work as long as there are resources for NT to adjust. For instance, if your system is experiencing a high cache miss rate, NT can improve this only if there is memory available to increase the cache size.

Monitoring and Adjusting Your Network

NT's network tools can be used to monitor your system and track the use of its resources. The Performance Monitor is the primary tool for monitoring your system's resources. Remember that it is important to accumulate baseline data for your system in order to know what changes to make. Performance Monitor is covered in more detail in Chapters 6 and 7. This short section will focus on how to use Performance Monitor to monitor network type objects.

A number of parameters in Performance Monitor relate to network performance. Native NT provides a number of standard parameters and is built so that other vendors can add their own parameters for their protocols. For instance, Pathworks for Windows NT plugs into Performance Monitor, allowing Pathworks-specific parameters to be monitored along with NT's native parameters. This allows you to plot both NT parameters and vendor-specific parameters on the same graphs, making problem areas easy to diagnose.

You can also set up alerts with Performance Monitor that can trigger specific actions when the alert trigger occurs. This action can be sending a message to a user or system or executing a program that carries out a specific action. Alerts are a great tool when you are concerned about a specific parameter or problem.

You can also force Performance Monitor to stay on top of all other applications by selecting the Always on Top option. Selecting Always on Top and resizing the window to a small corner of the screen lets you continue to work and still keep an eye on the system.

Performance Monitor can also monitor the performance of other machines on your network. The Computer Name field found in Performance Monitor and many other NT applications allows you to select any other NT-compatible system on the network.

Event Viewer can also monitor network events on any NT-compatible system on the network. Event Viewer displays and logs events that occur in the system and application programs. NT's network software and other vendor's software will write events in the event logs using the exception-handling systems of NT. Event Viewer is covered in more detail in Chapters 6 and 8.

Typical events relating to network problems will be logged by the network services on your system. This may be NT services or vendor network services such as DECnet, IPX, or LAT.

Events may relate to network problems, security issues or application problems. For instance, File Manager can be used to set up security auditing for files on your system. As security-related events occur, they will be recorded in the Security log, which you can access from Event Viewer. User Manager is used to set up auditing for each NT system. Once auditing is turned on, the audited events will show up in the Event Viewer.

Event Viewer provides options for filtering, sorting, and other controls for each log. Event Viewer is covered in more detail in Chapter 6.

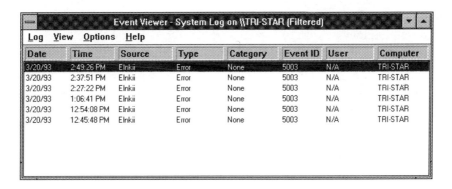

Event Viewer with Network Events

The Control Panel also provides the Server applet, which is useful for managing network resources on your NT system. The types of information that this applet can monitor and control include:

◆ The number and details of user sessions.

◆ Shared resources.

◆ File usage by user.

◆ Directory replication.

◆ The network destinations of alerts.

The following figure illustrates the dialog from the Server applet. Notice that along with the buttons that bring up the detail dialogs, it also contains a summary of current activity on the system.

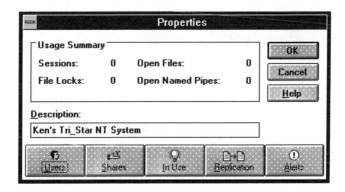

Server Applet

Remember when using the Server applet that the information relates to the total system. In other words, some of the information is related to network usage, while other information may pertain to local usage. For instance, if you are looking at print jobs, the jobs may be part local and the balance from network users.

The Users button displays a dialog showing the users connected to your system and the files they have open. Click on a user, and his or her open files will be displayed in the lower box.

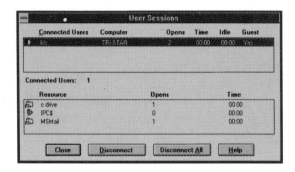

User Sessions Dialog

The Connected Users information shows the current users, the time they have been connected, and the resources they are using.

The Share Resources button brings up the following dialog, which shows the Shares on the system and the connected users, plus lots of other information.

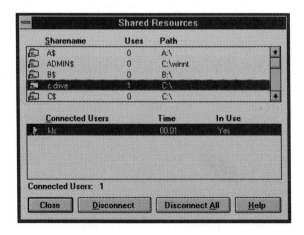

Shared Resources Dialog

Both of these applets are extremely useful and dangerous, because you not only can view information on network shares, but you can also disconnect one or more users from your system. Disconnecting a user from a resource may cause the loss of data if the user's application has made changes that have not been saved. Disconnecting a user could corrupt a file if the application is in the midst of performing an update that does not have rollback or recovery capabilities.

The Alert button brings up the Alerts dialog illustrated below. This dialog allows you to add or remove systems and users that will be sent administrative alerts for the system.

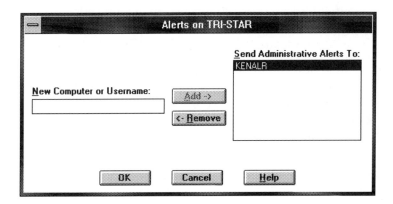

Server Alert Dialog

In the figure above, the box on the right lists the current systems or users that will receive alert messages. To add a new recipient, simply enter the system's name in the New Computer or User name box and click Add. To remove a system or user, highlight the name in the right box and click Remove.

Chapter 6 offers more information about these applets.

Troubleshooting Your Network

Any time you connect two or more systems together and form a network, you will have problems at some point. The extent of the problems will be a factor of how complex the network is, the number of applications and protocols used, the quality of hardware used, and the cable plant of the network. The sophistication of your users and the traffic on your network also factor into the number of problems you will experience.

Problems with Shared Connections

The most frequent network problems you will experience with your NT system will probably relate to accessing shared resources. One of the most frequent problem with shared resources is the cable system. This includes connectors that are pulled loose or poorly installed; cables that are not properly installed or are close to sources of interference, such as fluorescent lights, radio antennas, or large electric motors; active network components, such as bridges and routers; or problems with your network interface card. PC problems can also cause problems with shared resources. If a network problem occurs on a PC sharing resources, the resources will either disconnect or possibly exhibit intermittent problems.

Shared resources that provide poor performance are an indication of a loading problem on the network or workstations sharing the resources, a software setting on the shared systems, or possibly a problem with a piece of network hardware or software.

The first place to check is the workstation sharing the resource. If a large number of other users are using the resource at the same time or if the workstation has a lot of other processes running, the workstation may be overloaded. NT provides a number of tools for checking which resources are being used and who is using them. The Control Panel Server applet provides access to which users are using your system and what resources they are using. The Control Panel Network applet is used to add and configure network components.

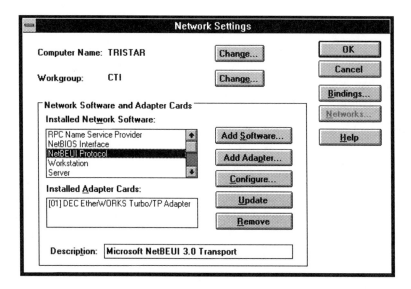

Control Panel Network Applet

The Control Panel Network applet allows you to change the settings of various network software and hardware components. We are going to look at the NetBEUI and Server settings, because we are concerned with the performance of shared resources. Select the NetBEUI protocol and click Configure (or double-click NetBEUI) to display the following dialog.

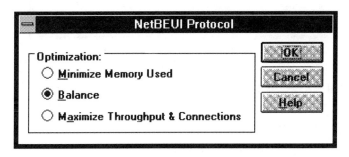

Protocol Settings Dialog

The NetBEUI Protocol dialog provides three buttons that control the performance of the protocol. The default setting is Balance, which provides a balance between network performance and memory usage on the workstation. If your system is primarily a server, selecting Maximize Connections will improve the performance of shared resources. The buttons are defined in the following table.

Option	Description
Minimize Memory Used	Selecting this option restricts the maximum number of connections to ten.
Balance	The Balance option allows up to sixty-four connections.
Maximize Throughput and Connections	This option allows more than sixty-four connections.

The server is configured in the same manner as the NetBEUI protocol: Select the Server from the list of installed network software and click Configure (or double-click Server).

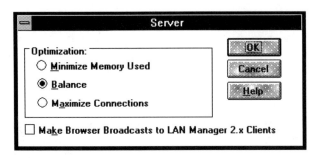

Server Settings Dialog

The Server dialog contains the same three Optimization buttons as the NetBEUI Protocol dialog and adds a check box for LAN Manager V2.x networks. Refer to the NetBEUI discussion above for tips on setting the Optimization buttons.

The Make Browser Broadcasts to LAN Manager 2.x Clients should be selected only if your network has LAN Manager V2.x clients and/or servers on your network. Turning on this option will cause the server to broadcast messages to 2.x systems that will allow them to browse shared resources on your system. If you don't need this option, turn it off to reduce network overhead on the system.

Other tools such as Performance Monitor and Event Viewer can be used for monitoring other parts of the system and for displaying event information concerning events that take place on your network.

A wide variety of problems can occur with sharing resources, ranging from reduced local performance to resources that cannot be shared or that suddenly disconnect when users access the service.

Failure to Access a Shared Resource at Startup

Accessing a shared connection when NT boots requires that the NT workstation and the workstation sharing the resource both boot and connect to the network correctly. If either machine fails to connect to the network, problems will occur.

Resources cannot be shared unless the sharing workstation is properly connected. If an error occurs in this workstation's boot process, no other workstations will be able to access its resources. Likewise, a workstation must successfully connect to the network before it can access resources on other workstations. The following checklist provides suggestions for tracking down problems related to other systems connecting to shared resources on your system.

Check	No	Yes
Can your workstation access resources on other workstations?	Continue Checklist.	Check the other workstations' network connection and password/resource names.
Are the network drivers loading during startup?	Check the Event Viewer for errors and correct any problems.	Call Microsoft Technical Support.

You should also make sure the shared resource has not reached the user limit for the resource.

Failure to Connect to Other Resources at Startup

NT's failure to share a resource when it boots is very similar to the failure to connect to a shared resource at startup. You should make sure you can connect to resources on any machine on the network. If you can connect to resources on a machine other than the one that has the problem, the problem is most likely on that machine. If you can't connect to resources on any machine, check out the network cable system. This is especially true if your system does not appear to have problems sharing resources, but others can't connect to resources on your machine.

Losing a Shared Connection

A shared connection can be lost as a result of a number of occurrences. The most frequent reason for losing a shared connection is common to any peer-to-peer network: Someone either disables sharing of the shared service or restarts or powers down the workstation sharing the resource. If sharing is halted on a machine that is sharing resources, all the shared resources will also be dropped.

Unable to Share a Resource

If your workstation can't share a resource, it is usually a problem with the workstation that can't share the resource. For instance, the following message appears if you try to share a resource and the Workstation service has not been started.

Error Dialog from Trying to Share a Resource

REMOTE ACCESS TO NT

Remote access to NT systems is provided as a standard NT feature by the Remote Access Service (RAS). The NT Desktop package allows one connection via RAS, while NT Advanced Server supports multiple simultaneous connections.

RAS allows a workstation such as a notebook or home system to connect to an NT system via a telephone connection. The connection may be through a dialup or dedicated line. A dedicated line is the preferred method, because it is a permanent connection from one system to another, but dedicated lines are usually expensive.

RAS also supports access via the X.25 protocol. X.25 services allow you to connect to an NT system using public carriers such as Sprintnet.

For more information about setting up and using RAS, consult your NT documentation.

MANAGING AND USING OTHER NETWORKS WITH NT

NT provides a foundation for other networks and network applications. Multiple protocols can be installed and running at the same time under NT. This is evidenced by NetBEUI and TCP/IP, which ship with NT. Installing other networks such as Pathworks and NetWare allows NT systems to run all the protocols simultaneously and participate in each network at the same time. For instance, an NT workstation/server can access resources on a Pathworks server, a NetWare server, and other NT servers and share resources at the same time.

This section will focus on Pathworks for Windows NT and NetWare and cover how to install other networks. We will also look at how these other networks can provide benefits to your organization and discuss the features of each.

Pathworks for Windows NT

Pathworks for Windows NT demonstrates the expandability of NT and is a part of Digital's NAS environment. The Pathworks product family has always been one of the few networks that provided a real foundation for integrated corporate networks. The Pathworks family supports NT, ULTRIX, SCO UNIX, OS/2, and OpenVMS servers, as well as DOS, Windows, Macintosh, OS/2, and NT clients.

Pathworks for Windows NT allows current Pathworks networks to take advantage of the features of NT and continue to use their current network. Installing Pathworks for Windows NT turns the machine into both a client and a server for your network. Any NT workstation with a Pathworks for Windows NT license can attach to any Pathworks server on the network. The same machine can also share services with other NT-compatible clients and other Pathworks clients.

Pathworks for Windows NT offers a nice option for expanding your existing network when performance becomes an issue. Installing an AXP or Intel NT machine and loading Pathworks for Windows NT is a very-low cost addition to your server arsenal. Because existing clients can access the server's resources, you can move file and print resources to the new NT server, freeing up resources on existing servers. NT's ease of installation (similar to that of Windows V3.1) and the ease with which Pathworks is installed on NT makes the addition of the NT server very simple.

Non-Pathworks clients can connect to Pathworks for Windows NT servers using NetBEUI or TCP/IP.

Client/Server Applications

Digital has been in the client/server business for many years. The VAX and OpenVMS product lines have pioneered network and client/server technologies that have been used by a wide-ranging number of businesses. Pathworks for Windows NT supports such client/server applications as client/server database applications via SQL services and Microsoft's Open Database Connectivity (ODBC) standard.

Digital and third-party vendors provide a wide variety of products that NT systems can access. These products include electronic mail, image management, performance management, and others.

Protocols

Pathworks for Windows NT includes the DECnet protocol, allowing NT systems to participate as clients and servers in a DECnet network. DECnet features task-to-task communication, NetBIOS API support, network file transfer applications, a job spawner utility, and the file access listener utility.

Pathworks for Windows NT systems can also use NetBEUI and TCP/IP simultaneously.

DOS Binary Compatibility for Pathworks Applications

Pathworks for Windows NT is binary compatible with DOS and Windows V3.x Pathworks applications. This allows you to leverage your investment in these applications as you move into the future with new Win32 applications.

Additional Network Features

The new FDDI EISA card from Digital is supported for TCP/IP and DECnet. This card lets NT systems access FDDI networks as both a client and a server.

Pathworks for Windows NT provides dialup access to NT systems through asynchronous DECnet. Asynchronous DECnet allows other systems to access NT resources through dialup lines. This is very handy for travelers and remote offices.

Management Tools

NT's management tools have been reviewed in this and other chapters. You should have an appreciation of the power that NT brings to workstation and network management. Pathworks for Windows NT demonstrates how other applications can take advantage of this power and plug in to NT's management system.

Pathworks for Windows NT integrates into the Performance Monitor and Event Logger. Integrating into these applications provides other networks such as Pathworks with complete tools for monitoring performance and logging events and provides the NT user or manager with one set of tools to use on a workstation or server.

Pathworks for Windows NT also provides management support for managing other DECnet nodes. NT systems can also be remotely managed by Digital's Polycenter systems using SNMP services.

Pathworks for Windows NT Installation

The Pathworks for NT software is shipped on diskette. The installation process is straightforward and can install an NT server, an NT client, or both.

1. Log in as administrator.

2. Select the Networks applet in Control Panel.

3. Click Add Software.

4. Select Other Network Software from the list of options.

5. Click Continue.

6. Enter the drive where the Pathworks distribution files are located and click OK.

7. Select Pathworks from the OEM option dialog and click OK.

8. Click Continue.

9. Enter Y or N to the View Release notes dialog. If you answered yes to the last prompt, close Notepad when you have finished reading the release notes.

10. Click Continue, and the installation will be completed.

After the installation is complete, the Network dialog will reappear. The following steps will configure Pathworks for NT:

1. Select Pathworks for NT from the list of installed software.

2. Click Configure.

3. Enter the node name, node address, and adapter type in the following dialog. (Note that this dialog is from an early version and will probably change slightly for shipping versions of Pathworks for Windows NT.)

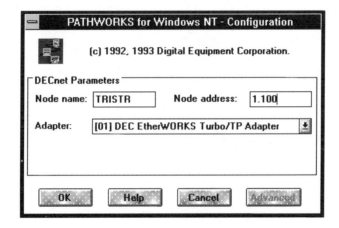

4. Click OK.

When the Restart System dialog appears, select Reboot Now. After NT restarts, Pathworks should be running.

Novell NetWare

NT will work cleanly in a NetWare environment because of NT's support for networks as part of its open architecture. NT can perform as a NetWare client and a NT server at the same time. NT and Windows for Workgroups clients can access both NT and NetWare servers simultaneously because of their support for multiple network protocols.

The NetWare drivers for NT are available direct from Novell and are also on CompuServe in the NetWare forum. Microsoft may at some time bundle the drivers in the NT package, but this is uncertain at this time.

CHAPTER 5

The Windows NT Architecture

The introduction of NT brings an interesting twist to the computer systems market. Before NT, the question was whether to use this or that operating system and interface on this particular hardware and how to integrate these systems with other more powerful systems such as OpenVMS or UNIX workstations and timesharing systems. NT is the first system since the introduction of OpenVMS to provide a clear growth path from desktop machines to more powerful systems used as servers or multiuser systems.

Because NT will run end-user applications, such as DOS and traditional Windows, on any hardware platform, a clear and safe growth path is established for almost any standalone or network system.

NT also introduces a new file system called NTFS. This is a robust file system that supports long file names, sophisticated security features, and advanced file-recovery procedures. NTFS and LAN Manager for NT also supports disk striping, mirroring, and other features that are expected of an advanced operating system.

SUPPORT FOR STANDARDS

NT was designed to support numerous standards from its inception. One of the primary goals was to make the moving of existing 16-bit Windows applications to Windows NT as easy as possible. Supported standards include support for traditional applications, such as POSIX, Windows V3.x, and DOS, and extended applications, such as multimedia, database, and programming. For instance, the Win32 API was supported first in Windows NT and eventually moved to the standard Windows product via the Win32S API.

By supporting these standards, NT will run programs written for the specific environments. DOS, POSIX, and Windows V3.x programs will run on any NT machine, regardless of which type of processor the machine uses.

This hardware independence makes life much easier for managers, because they can invest in the technology required for a particular job and not be concerned with whether it has an Intel processor or not.

NT will support other standards that have been introduced by Microsoft and other organizations. For instance, the machine I am using now runs NT and contains a VL VESA bus. The VESA bus is used by the video card and a high-performance SCSI controller. NT supports this hardware standard by using a special driver from the graphics card manufacturer. Other standards that NT supports include ODBC, Messaging Application Program Interface (MAPI), WIN32 API, and the Simple Network Management Protocol (SNMP).

Multiple networking standards are also supported by NT. The NT distribution kit includes TCP/IP and NetBEUI. Third-party products are adding standard support for such protocols as DECnet and IPX. For more information, see Chapter 4.

Portability

Hardware portability is a buzzword that has been kicked around in the UNIX community for many years. The problem is, it has been very difficult to obtain. NT addresses this problem by moving the hardware-specific functions into the Hardware Abstraction Layer (HAL). HAL isolates the NT executive from the hardware services, making NT easier to port to different hardware platforms. In most instances, only the HAL code must be changed to move NT to a new platform. The first hardware platforms to support NT include:

- ◆ Digital's Alpha AXP.

- ◆ Mips Technologies Inc.'s R4xxx.

- ◆ Intel's Pentium.

- ◆ Intel's 386 and 486.

There are plans to port NT to additional platforms as other vendors scramble to climb on board the NT train.

NT portability also goes beyond just the processor type. Because NT is a multiprocessing system, the ability to run on different types of hardware becomes even more important. The difference between a 66-MHz 486 and a 100-MHz RISC machine may not sound like much, but what happens when one or the other is a multiprocessor machine with two or more processors? The performance difference becomes drastic. For example, a two-processor 66-MHz PC is 132-MHz, right? Now think of a multiprocessor AXP PC: 150 MHz x 2 = 300 MHz. I suspect the actual performance difference will be close to 100 percent, because NT will evenly distribute threads over two or more distinct paths. The actual gains will depend on what tasks are being performed on the machine.

Memory Model

Windows NT uses a flat 32-bit memory model that banishes the 640-KB limits of DOS. The total address space for any NT application is 4 GB using virtual memory. Both physical and virtual memory is organized into pages of 4 KB.

Full memory protection is included for every concurrently executing process in the NT system. Win32 supports both global memory (visible by all processes) and local memory (visible to the calling process only). The memory-protection features of Win32 prevent applications from overwriting or reading memory of other applications. This protection was proven many times during the beta testing when I managed to blow up a number of DOS or Windows V3.1 applications and some NT applications. From the October 1992 beta release on, none of these applications caused problems for NT when they blew up. The application simply went away, but NT kept humming merrily along. The same cannot be said for Windows V3.1 or Windows for Workgroups V3.1, which can still lock up entirely when an application goes out, depending on what the application is doing.

Multitasking

Windows NT is a pre-emptive multitasking operating system that divides up the CPU time among the different process operating at any given moment. The operating system scheduler is pre-emptive, gaining control whenever a clock interrupt occurs, allowing NT to take control of the processor at any time, whether or not the currently executing process will yield control. The scheduler determines which process gets the next available CPU cycles by reviewing the priority of the processes waiting to execute.

Windows NT also supports multithreaded applications by providing a multithreaded process structure. This provides an ideal environment for programs that are CPU intensive, because the intensive tasks can be split off into their own process. Minicomputer programs have been doing this for years with programs such as Finite Element Analysis processors.

Multiple threads of execution may occur within any process, including threads running on the same processor or on different processors in a multiprocessor machine.

The priority of processes falls into one of three classes: high, normal, or idle. The default priority of a process is set to normal. Within each class there are five priority levels. The scheduler can override the priority of a process by changing the process's dynamic priority. This usually occurs when certain system events take place, such as when a window gains focus or a process waiting for an I/O event has the wait satisfied.

Multiprocessor Support

NT is a symmetric multiprocessing (SMP) system, that is, it can execute one or more processors simultaneously. NT can also share its memory between processes running on any processor on a multiprocessor (MP) machine. The interprocess communication capabilities of NT make life easier for programmers that wish to write multithreaded applications to take advantage NT's SMP support.

The SMP features of NT are automatically implemented by NT and do not require any special handing of a program. NT can run any part of the operating system (except for the kernel) and all application programs on multiple processors. Multithreaded applications will be split across multiple processors, drastically increasing the performance of the application. All of this, and the developer may not even know the application is running on an MP machine.

The NT Desktop package will support systems with one or two processors. Versions of NT Desktop for systems with more than two processors will be offered directly from OEMs.

NT Advanced Server will support up to four processors. OEMs will also offer their own versions of this package for systems with more than four processors.

Device Drivers

Windows NT device drivers are typically code libraries that provide access to devices such as disk and network I/O. Windows NT device drivers are usually layered, with one driver providing the generic support, such as a generic SCSI driver, and other small drivers providing specific support for a particular adapter. Developing device drivers for Windows NT will be much easier, because developers can concentrate on the specifics of their device and use the generic services of the general driver. Applications can also rely on a standard interface to services such as network interfaces and scanners.

A neat feature of NT is the ability to dynamically load and unload device drivers while Windows NT is running.

Dynamic Link Library

A dynamic link library (DLL) is similar to an object library or subroutine library in traditional programming environments. The major difference in DLLs is how they are dynamically linked at run time instead of compile time. A DLL is actually a separate file containing a collection of subroutines that may be called at any time. The DLL does not use any system resources, other than disk space, until it is called.

NT uses DLLs to handle many of the features of the operating system. Security, file systems, and so on, are handled by numerous DLLs explicitly designed for each task.

Network Support

Windows NT provides many generic functions for accessing and controlling network services. The network functions are not network specific, providing support for adding, canceling, and retrieving information about network connections for different networks.

NT's support for networks includes NetBIOS compatibility for applications requiring this functionality.

Memory-Mapped File I/O

The memory-mapped file facility of NT provides a mechanism for applications to map a file to memory and treat the file as if it is truly memory. Word processors and spreadsheets are examples of programs that could really take advantage of this feature. The process of mapping a file creates a named area of memory that corresponds to the file.

Programs that must share data may also take advantage of memory mapping by using a common mapped file. Mapped files provide a nice facility for sharing data because the data is actually written to disk and not just stored in memory.

A memory-mapped file is loaded into virtual memory and may be paged with I/O caching. This allows programmers to treat a file as if it were loaded entirely in memory, freeing them from the time-consuming task of reinventing the wheel for these tasks. Since the mapping is handled by the operating system, it should offer improved performance over programs that handle this internally. Programs that are very file intensive, such as graphics and multimedia, should especially benefit from this I/O feature. New versions of NT should also improve the performance of programs that use memory mapping, as NT has improvements made to the memory mapping and paging facilities.

Serial Ports

NT supports up to 256 serial ports! The ports retain the normal DOS device names, COM1 - COM256. Serial port configurations are managed by the Ports applet in Control Panel.

NT removes many of the serial port restrictions that we have lived with for years. x86 systems typically support up to four serial ports. Many applications have problems with serial devices above COM2 because of the way DOS and Windows V3.x handle the serial ports.

Worldwide Language Support

Windows NT supports the 16-bit Unicode character set, which includes all the world's alphabets. Support for the Unicode allows Windows NT to be configured for any local language around the world.

Applications can easily be designed to work in any language. Any NT application can be quickly translated to and from any other language, even those with radically different structures, such as Western and Far East languages. Language support is provided by a resource file mechanism that allows translation to another language without changes to an application's source code.

Character-Based Applications

NT provides support for character-based applications by providing a console interface. The NT console displays output in a window that emulates a terminal display. The console interface supports standard input, output, and error operations. Redirection of input and output is handled through pipes and files in a manner similar to that of DOS and UNIX.

Unlike a typical terminal, an NT console can be shared by a group of processes. Because of NT's multithreaded capability, a character-mode application can create subprocesses that also share the same output window. The standard input/output devices are defined as:

StdIn   CONIN$

StdOut   CONOUT$

StdErr   CONOUT$

NT Environment Subsystems

NT uses environment subsystems to implement support for user interfaces. Environment subsystems allow NT to support new functionality by adding a new subsystem without making changes to NT internals.

The Win32 subsystem handles screen, mouse, and keyboard services for all other subsystems. Win32 is the only environment subsystem that is shared by all environment subsystems. This is because all other subsystems use Win32 for screen, mouse, and keyboard services.

The MS-DOS environment is supported through a Virtual DOS Machine (VDM). A VDM can be thought of as a complete 386/486 computer implemented in software. Every VDM is protected from other programs by running in its own address space.

All Win16 programs are run in a single VDM. Win16 programs multitask as they would on Windows V3.x, because only one Win16 program can run at one time, while all other Win16 programs will be blocked.

The POSIX interface is implemented as a separate subsystem. POSIX support in the initial release of NT is limited to IEEE 100V3.1-1990 applications.

The third major subsystem delivered with Windows NT will support OS/2 V1.x character-based programs.

Both the POSIX and OS/2 subsystems are automatically loaded when NT boots, but are swapped to disk until their services are required by a program.

GRAPHICS

Enhanced metafiles are a new metafile format introduced with NT. An enhanced metafile will maintain its appearance on any device, either hardcopy or on a Win32 screen. Enhanced metafiles store enough information to reproduce the image correctly on any other device. This additional information also includes optional entries for a description, author name, date of creation and so on.

EVENT LOGGING

Event logs are used by NT to store records of interesting system events. These events may occur with the NT system or within third-party applications. The third-party event-logging support provides applications with the ability to trap and record program events in a standardized manner. All events may be reviewed by using the NT Event Viewer.

EXCEPTION HANDLING

NT provides a structured exception-handling architecture for handling software and hardware errors. Errors can be trapped and reported to the calling system, allowing it to take the appropriate action.

SECURITY ACCOUNTS MANAGER

The Security Accounts Manager (SAM) database is used to store account names and passwords. A local SAM database is automatically maintained on each NT system as user accounts are added and changed.

The SAM database is accessed each time a user logs in to a workstation as the NT security subsystem validates the username and password.

LAN Manager for NT systems can have an additional SAM database maintained by a Domain Controller. Users may choose to log in to a local workstation or domain at login time. Domain controllers simplify account management by keeping all user accounts for the domain in one place. Logging in to the domain provides access to all the services in the domain to which you have access.

SERVICE CONTROL MANAGER

The Service Control Manager (SCM) provides a comprehensive and secure means of controlling services installed on an NT system. SCM maintains a service database that is part of the NT registry. Information stored in the SCM database includes the name of the program, the status information for each service, automatic startup specifications, the user logon account for the service, a dependency list of other services and drivers, and other related information. Services stored in the SCM database can be either a Win32 or a driver service.

The SCM database consists of two different databases: ServicesActive and ServicesFailed. ServicesActive contains information about the currently installed services. The ServicesFailed database contains information about the SCM configuration when NT failed to boot, providing a valuable resource for troubleshooting problems with booting an NT system. If you have ever changed Windows V3.1's SYSTEM.INI and were unable to reboot (and did not have a backup), you will really appreciate this feature.

A copy of the ServicesActive database is saved as a last-known-good database each time the ServicesActive database is modified. This provides NT with a fall-back boot configuration if it encounters a problem at boot time.

When NT boots, SCM loads services that are automatically loaded by using the ServicesActive database. If there is a problem because a critical service will not start, NT will automatically reboot the system. Before performing the reboot, NT will set ServicesFailed to point to the failed database and ServicesActive to point to the last-known-good database. NT also has provisions for ignoring all SCM boot services if the last-known-good database will still not start. In this situation, NT will usually boot to some minimum configuration.

SCM also maintains the status of each service after it is started. Win32 services communicate with SCM when status changes occur to the service, while SCM must query driver services for status information. The SCM database also includes information about some services that are started before the SCM. When SCM tries to start these services, it will receive a message that the service is already running. SCM then updates the status of the services and continues to load other services.

Date and Time Services

NT uses two date and time formats. The format used for maintaining times on files (file time) uses two 32-bit values as a combined 64-bit value. The time represents the number of 100-nanosecond intervals that have elapsed since January 1, 1601. The standard system time (system time) consists of separate values for year, month, day, hour, minute, second, and millisecond.

Multimedia

NT carries forward the multimedia support that appeared in Windows V3.0 and was integrated into V3.1. Because of NT's support for extremely powerful hardware platforms, multimedia should really take off with NT. These powerful processors will provide the power requirements to extend multimedia into day-to-day activities that can benefit from the technology, including presentations, real-time conferencing, and multimedia databases.

The MMSYSTEM library provides media control interface services and low-level multimedia services. Device drivers provide the interface between MMSYSTEM and the multimedia devices. Because the device drivers are implemented as DLLs, they use run-time links to multimedia programs, providing a clean path for upgrading MMSYSTEM or the driver separately, or both together. MMSYSTEM was designed as an extensible interface and to isolate applications from the device drivers.

CONFIGURATION CONTROL

Let's first look at the NT Registry and then begin to look at specific features of the NT architecture that make life easier for us.

The Registry is used for storing configuration information about a workstation. The Registry is a centralized database that is accessible both locally from the current workstation and remotely over a network. The Registry is used to store many types of information, including user preferences such as desktop settings and personal group settings; configuration specifications such as drivers; and performance data.

The Registry is a real-time database that NT uses for many tasks. For instance, real-time performance data is kept in the Registry. This simplifies the process of saving the data, since the Registry is always open and accessible to NT, and makes retrieving the data a snap. The same NT functions that access other Registry data can manipulate performance data as well. The registry files are stored in \WINNT\SYSTEM32\CONFIG.

Many Windows applications and utilities, such as NT Setup, Control Panel, PIF Editor, and Print Manager, use and update information in the Registry. NT also includes utility called REGEDIT32 that can be used by experienced users to directly change the Registry. Be careful with REGEDIT32, because improper use can cause major headaches for your system. NT fortunately stores a copy of the most recent successful Registry for cases in which you trash your system. When NT encounters a system boot problem that it cannot work around, it uses the last good copy of the Registry to boot the system.

The Registry begins the siren call for the old standby files such as AUTOEXEC.BAT, CONFIG.SYS, and the great number of INI files in use today. We will see these files used for some time because of the great number of applications using them. Over time the information in INI files should move into the Registry, along with information in the AUTOEXEC.BAT and CONFIG.SYS files.

The Registry stores information by different keys, including the four predefined keys:

Registry Key	Description
HKEY_USERS	HKEY_USERS is the root of all user profiles on the computer.
HKEY_CURRENT_USER	HKEY_CURRENT_USER is the root of the configuration information for the current user and is a subkey of HKEY_USERS. Their user's Profile is stored under this key (Program Manager groups, screen colors, and control panel settings).
HKEY_LOCAL_MACHINE	HKEY_LOCAL_MACHINE contains configuration information particular to the computer system. This information is for all users.
HKEY_CLASSES_ROOT	HKEY_CLASSES_ROOT stores information relating to file associations (File/Associate in File Manager) and is a subkey of HKEY_LOCAL_MACHINE. Object Linking and Embedding (OLE) information is also stored under this key.

The Registry is used for storing all kinds of information about NT and NT services. The following snapshot of the REGEDIT window shows the Registry entry for a network connection to another system, in this case a Windows for Workgroups system named DELL320.

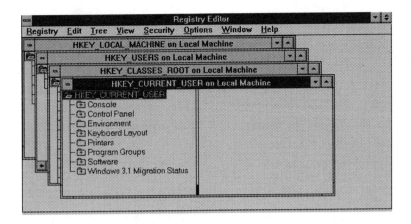

REGEDIT Main Window

Boot Configuration Files

Configuration Files

NT has numerous fault-tolerant features, including a critical boot-friendly feature for anyone who has dinked with CONFIG.SYS on a DOS machine and was unable to boot the PC. NT automatically keeps a copy of the last known good boot configuration for your system. If NT cannot boot using the current configuration, it will automatically warn you and switch to the old configuration.

A second helpful feature of NT is the ability of Setup to create a repair boot disk for your system. This disk can only be used if and when your boot configuration files becomes corrupted (for example, when there is a hard disk problem) so that NT cannot access critical information in the Registry.

Booting Multiple Operating Systems

NT supports multiple operating systems on the same system via the Flexboot feature. Flexboot allows any number of NT or other operating systems to be selected at boot time, with one restriction. MS-DOS and OS/2 systems require operating system files to be located in the root directory of the main drive. Because of this requirement, Flexboot supports only one root-based operating system, that is, either MS-DOS or OS/2, but not both.

Startup options can be changed by using the System applet (Control Panel).

Intel Systems

BOOT.INI is stored in the root directory of your system drive and contains minimal startup information for your system. An example BOOT.INI is shown below:

```
[FLEXBOOT]

TIMEOUT=30

DEFAULT=C:\

[OPERATING SYSTEMS]

MULTI(0)DISK(0)RDISK(0)PARTITION(1)\WINNTOCT =
"WINDOWS NT " /NODEBUG

C:\ = "MS-DOS ON C:\"
```

The information in BOOT.INI is used to define the operating systems and versions on your computer and provide information to the boot process about where system files are located and which system is the default.

The sample BOOT.INI above uses MS-DOS as the default operating system and sets a 30-second time-out value for selecting another system. In other words, you have 30 seconds in which to select NT in this example, or MS-DOS will automatically boot.

RISC Systems

Reduced instruction set computer (RISC) systems use a nonvolatile RAM to store the same type of information contained in BOOT.INI. The exact implementation will vary from vendor to vendor. Consult your system manuals for the specifics for your system.

UNIVERSAL NAMING CONVENTION

The Universal Naming Convention (UNC) is a naming convention for identifying shared resources, such as directories and printers, over a network. UNC is a convenient method because it specifies both the server and the shared resource in one statement. The UNC format is:

```
\\SERVER\RESOURCE
SERVER is the server where the resource is located.
RESOURCE is the shared resource.
```

UNC names can be used whenever you point to a device on a network. Many of the NT programs, including File Manager and Print Manager, will automatically display UNC names that have browsing capabilities. Other systems that do not have browsing, such as Pathworks V4.x, may require you to specify the entire UNC name.

At times, you may use only part of the UNC name. The following UNC name would point to all resources of a particular type on a server named TRI-STAR:

```
\\TRI_STAR
```

FILE SYSTEMS

NT offers many new file-oriented features for programmers. A complete set of file I/O routines have been added that directly correspond to the DOS functions. NT and all future versions of Windows will perform all file I/O without having to call functions from the operating system.

Supported File Systems

NT supports three file systems. NT examines a volume the first time the volume is accessed or whenever a new volume is placed in a floppy drive to determine the type of file system on the volume. All I/O to a volume is then managed by a DLL that supports that particular file system.

File system features, such as mirroring, transaction processing, and security, will vary depending on the type of file system. For instance, many security features are supported only on NTFS.

File Allocation Table

The DOS FAT file system is supported by NT for backward compatibility with DOS and Windows V3.1 systems. This is the same old FAT system that has endured through the various versions of DOS. Only FAT-style file names and conventions are supported.

High-Performance File System

NT supports HPFS to maintain compatibility with OS/2 systems that may share files with an NT system. This is particularly important in a network environment that uses OS/2 client or server machines and begins to implement NT systems.

NT File System

NTFS is a transaction-based file system that logs all file transactions. NTFS also automatically maps out bad sectors on-the-fly.

NTFS should forever break the barriers imposed by DOS and the FAT system. NTFS file names can be from one to 256 characters long. Multiple extensions separated by periods are also supported. File names can contain spaces and almost any other character. File names containing spaces must be referenced by including the entire name in quotes. Characters not allowed in NTFS file names are < > : * / \ | .

NTFS file names also support mixed case, but the case is not significant when searching for or using a file. The file names Project Number One.Joes Taco and PROJECT NUMBER ONE.JOES TACO are both valid file names that reference the same file.

NTFS tries to be as friendly as possible when creating files. When a file with a long file name is created, NT also builds a DOS-compatible name in the 8.3 format. DOS applications running under NT will use the DOS-compatible name when accessing the NT file. Be forewarned that when some DOS applications that use only FAT file names write an NTFS file with a long file name, the long name is destroyed and the file's permissions may be replaced with the default permissions. This occurs because many DOS applications delete a file and then write the entire file to perform an update operation. Because the application does not understand long file names, the long name is not used. If the application simply updates the data in the file, the long name will not be touched.

When DOS applications will be using NTFS files, make sure the first eight characters of the file contain as much significance as possible. Files that take advantage of the full-length file names can be unintelligible to users of DOS applications if the first six characters are not significant. The reason the first six and not the first eight characters are significant is because NTFS will resolve duplicate short file names by adding a unique suffix to the first six characters of the file name.

Wildcard Characters
The wildcard characters we have used so frequently in DOS operations have also changed. The * references one entire word in an NTFS name instead of the remainder of a name or extension. For instance, the DOS command DIR TEMP*1.DOC will return all files beginning with TEMP. The same command on an NT system will return only tiles that fit the pattern. The following example illustrates the advantages:

F:\>DIR /b"project art*.*

```
Project Art 2 Building.Guilford County
Project Art 3 Building.Guilford County
Project Art Building.Guilford County
```

F:\>DIR "project * art * Building.*

```
Project Art 2 Building.Guilford County
Project Art 3 Building.Guilford County
```

Notice how the second command lists only files that have a 2 or 3 inserted in the name. This is because NT is treating the digit as a separate word because we specified an * after art and before building. File naming conventions will become even more important with NTFS because of its versatility. Combining the digits with the word ART in our example will solve the problem. The following example shows the new names:

```
Project Art Building.Guilford County
Project Art_2 Building.Guilford County
Project Art_3 Building.Guilford County
```

The * also stands for a group of characters when used as the last character before a period or as the last character in the name. DIR "Project *.* will list all project files. When quotes are used around a file name, only the leading quote is required, unless you are specifying parameters after the file name, in which case the trailing quote is also required.

The new wildcard characteristics apply to all NT file systems, including the FAT system. Of course, your FAT files will not be longer than the 8.3 format we are used to and will contain no spaces, but the wildcards treat them just like NTFS files.

File Attributes

NT tracks a number of attributes about a file. These consist of things such as permissions, file names, last change date, and the file's owner and size. A file's attributes are created when the file is created and updated during the file's lifetime as the attributes change.

The owner of a file is also established as the user who created the file when the file is created. A file's owner always has total control over a file. This means that the owner can change permissions of a file and anything else, including the file's data. Remember that the creator of a file cannot be denied access to a file, because he or she can always change the permissions back.

An NTFS file also has a list of permissions attached to the file. This list is called an Access Control List (ACL). The name should sound familiar to OpenVMS users. The ACL is a list of users who have access to the file and the types of access they possess. The users in an ACL can be either user account or group names.

NT file permissions are used to control access to a file. NTFS only allows access to a file if a user has explicit access. The access can be through a permission for the user's account or if the user belongs to a group that has access to the file. A new file will generally inherit the file permissions that apply to its directory. This includes files that are copied into a new directory. NT does not allow administrators to access a file unless they have permission. Remember that an administrator can always gain access by taking ownership of the file. If an administrator has gained ownership of a file, you will have a clue to this fact the next time you see that you are no longer the file's owner.

NT has four standard permissions. These permissions are actually preconfigured groups of special permissions. The standard permissions will typically provide the control required. The standard file and directory permissions are shown below:

Standard File Permissions

Permission	Description
No Access	No access to the file. Overrides all other permissions.
Read Change	View or execute the file, view attributes. Read permission, change data in the file, and delete the file.
Full Access	Complete control. Read + change, change file permissions.
Special Access	Display the Special Access dialog.

Special File Permissions

Permission	Description
Read	View and copy the file, view attributes (cannot execute a program file).
Write	Change data in the file or append data to the file.
Execute	Execute a program file. User must also have Read to execute a batch file.
Delete	Delete the file.
Change	Change a file's permissions.
Take Ownership	Become the owner of a file.

Standard Directory Permissions

Permission	Description
No Access	No access to the directory. Overrides all other permissions.
List	List files in the directory.
Read	List, read files in the directory.
Add	Create files in the directory.
Add+Read	Add and Read permissions.
Change	Create, List, Change attributes for the directory.
Full Access	Complete control. All permissions plus change file permissions.

Special Directory Permissions

Permission	Description
Read	List files in the directory and view permissions.
Write	Create files in the directory and change directory permissions.
Execute	Traverse the directory structure (the Everybody group has the Bypass Traverse Checking Right).
Delete	Delete the directory (if it is empty).
Change Permission	Create, List, Change permissions for the directory.

You may wonder what happens when a user is granted permission to a directory or file by his or her username and by being the member of a group. When multiple permissions exist for a user, NT will combine all permissions for the user to get the total list of permissions. The only exception to this is the No Access permission, which overrides all other permissions.

Separate permissions are maintained in the directory permissions for existing files and new files created in the directory. These permissions are like the other permissions in that they are maintained by user or group.

CHAPTER 6

Windows NT Management

INTRODUCTION TO MANAGING NT

Management of an NT system will mean different things to every user and manager. Systems used in a small office or at home will require very minimal system management chores, possibly less than a Windows V3.1 system because that pesky old DOS will be gone. Network and power user systems will require substantially more management, depending on the tasks performed by the system.

Users of standalone systems may use only Control Panel and Print Manager for management tasks. Many of these users will perform tasks such as changing fonts, configuring ports, or changing the system time with Control Panel. They may also use Print Manager to perform limited printer management tasks.

Other systems may require slightly more management. This will usually occur when you add users to your system and/or add your system to a network.

You may also experience a growth in management tasks if you or one of your users is a power user. It will become obvious that you are becoming a power user when you try to squeeze one more piece of hardware or software into your system and begin talking about IRQs or memory addresses. At this point you will probably begin to explore the depths of several Control Panel applets, as well as other applications such as Event Viewer and Performance Monitor.

The focus of this chapter is on tasks that are fairly specific to NT. Tasks that are similar to Windows V3.1, such as managing fonts or changing desktop settings, may be mentioned, but only briefly. Most current users will be familiar with these tasks, and new users will find them very easy and straightforward.

Managing User Accounts

User Accounts
One of the changes that NT brings to the management of single-user computers is its management tools. Windows V3.1 and DOS did not provide any facilities for managing multiple users of a single machine and in fact made the task very difficult.

The first clue NT gives of its user management is the logon dialog that forces the user to enter a valid account name and password to gain access to the system. User accounts allow a manager to add security and control access to any machine. This is particularly important in cases in which several people use the same computer.

User Accounts

You should create user accounts for all users on an NT system, regardless of whether the system is attached to a network or not. This will simplify the management of your system by protecting a user's files and configurations. It also a good idea to use a separate management account from your normal day-to-day account. Separating management rights (administrator and power user) from your normal rights makes accidental destruction of the system slightly more difficult. The auditing and resource control features of NT will add to this control of your systems by allowing you to tailor access to the system's files and directories.

Users with accounts in the Administrators group must be very careful with their password. We know that letting others have your password is very dangerous, but another little problem occurs if you lose your password for the Administrator accounts. If you do not have access to an NT system with an account in the Administrators group, you will not be able to manage the system and may actually lose access to files on the system.

User accounts are maintained with the NT User Manager program located in the Administrative Program Manager group. User Manager is an easy-to-use program that handles management of user accounts, groups, and policies. Like other NT management programs, its features are controlled by the NT security system, limiting which users can perform certain actions.

NT Default User Accounts

The following accounts are automatically added when NT is installed:

Account	Description
Administrator	This account is a member of the Administrators account and is the initial management account for the NT system. It cannot be removed from the Administrators group or deleted.
Guest	The Guest account is a member of the Guests group. The account cannot be deleted, but you can remove access to resources from the group, which prevents access to any resources by the account. You can also place a password on the group.
Initial User	The Initial User account is created during installation (unless the workstation is added to a domain) and is a member of the Administrators group.

User Account Names and Passwords

User accounts are used by NT to identify a user that tries to access the system. Each time a user tries to log in, he or she must enter a valid username and password. This is the same approach that is used by almost all LANs and multiuser systems. The username can be from one to twenty characters in length. A username can contain all characters except * [ ] + : ; " < > . , ?/\ |.

The username is an alphanumeric identifier that is linked to a numeric account number. The account number is never displayed to a user and is used by NT to identify the user. The NT documentation points out that an account number will never be reused, even if you delete a user account and create an account with the same name.

The password for a username can be from the minimum password length setting to fourteen characters in length. The password can contain alphanumeric and special characters and is case-sensitive. You must use care in entering a password, because a slip up can enter a mixed-case password that is very difficult to rediscover.

User Preferences

Windows has always been friendly in its user interface because of its ease of use and the ability of Windows and most programs to store a user's preferences of how a particular program behaves. The number and type of preferences saved depends on each program and may change greatly from one application to another.

NT adds to this capability by storing preferences for each user and allowing managers to set up common preferences for such things as program manager groups. The preferences are stored in the Registry, as described in Chapter 5. The standard preferences stored by user are: Printer selections; Control Panel settings for colors, mouse, sound, international settings, keyboard, and user environment variables; Program Manager groups and Save On Exit settings; File Manager Save On Exit settings; command prompt window settings; Print Manager connections and settings; NT Help bookmarks; and application settings that are saved in the Registry by the application. Note that all applications do not save settings in the Registry. The application must use NT systems services to save its settings in the Registry instead of INI files.

Storing all this information in a single database means that eventually your hard disk will not be filled with INI files that may or may not have any significance to you or other users. Having all this information in the Registry also means that you have only one set of information to back up instead of a multitude of INI and configuration files spread all over your disk drives.

Storing preferences by user secures the preferences for each user from being destroyed by others. It will also reduce the support calls for preference-related questions.

Program Manager Groups

Common Program Manager groups are shared by all users on an NT system. Applications and files that are security-sensitive or for some other reason should not be shared should be placed in Personal groups. Personal groups are specific to a particular user and are tied to that user's ID code.

The File/New menu command is used to create both Common and Personal groups and to place items in either type of group. When you select File New, the following dialog is displayed.

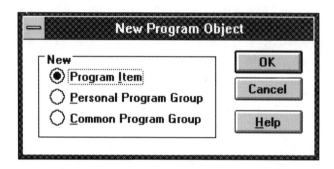

New Program Object Dialog

To create a new group, click on Personal Program Group or Common Program Group and click OK. Enter the name for the group in the next dialog and again click OK. The process is just as easy as creating a group under Windows V3.1, except when creating groups for multiple users.

NT uses two icons to represent minimized groups. The icons quickly identify which groups are Personal or Common. While the icons help in quickly spotting which groups are Personal or Common, this works only if the groups are minimized, because there is no indicator on a nonminimized group whether it is Personal or Common.

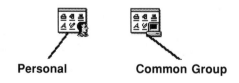

Personal   **Common Group**

Personal and Common Group Icons

Let's say that you create accounts for ten users on your NT system. Each of these users needs a common set of applications but also requires several special groups. The Common groups can be created by logging in as Administrator and creating them as Common groups. Each Personal group, however, must be created separately. To create a Personal group, you must log in as that user and create the group as a Personal group. There is also no easy way to copy a group from one user to another.

User Groups

User groups are provided by most networks and many operating systems to simplify the management of the system's resources. NT continues this trend by providing facilities for the creation and management of User groups. A group is simply a way of lumping a number of users into the same category to control access to some aspect of the system. For example, you might create a group for each department in your organization. The groups would typically be given access to resources that should be shared by the group. Other groups might be created to allow access to resources that are shared across departments.

Groups are also useful for controlling management of your NT system. NT has two special groups that relate to the management of accounts: Administrators and Power Users. The Administrators group gives a user account the ability to manage or access anything on the system. The Power Users group is slightly less powerful than the Administrators. For instance, power users can manage all user accounts and groups they created in User Manager, except those of administrators.

The Power Users and Administrators groups also provide a number of other privileges to users. Power users can share resources such as directories and printers, install and manage printers, and set the system time. Power users cannot perform such tasks as formatting a disk, backing up and restoring the system, or doing system-level debugging, among others. Administrators can perform any function on the system. The Administrators group or account is roughly equivalent to the SYSTEM account of an OpenVMS system or the ROOT account of a UNIX system.

Groups that are created on a standalone system or a workstation that is attached to a network are called local groups. These groups can contain only permissions for resources on the workstation, not on other workstations on the network. Local groups can contain user accounts of network users only if the workstation is part of a LAN Manager domain.

Global groups are another type of group that can be granted access to resources on other systems and a local workstation. Global groups can be created and maintained only in LAN Manager domains. Global groups can also become members of Local groups on a workstation, giving the Global group access to all the resources in the workstation group.

Groups should be used for managing most resources on all NT systems. This will not only simplify the management of your systems but will also provide for easy integration of the system into a LAN manager domain.

NT comes with several predefined groups that are used to tailor the actions of NT. The default groups are:

- ◆ Users.
- ◆ Power Users.
- ◆ Administrators.
- ◆ Backup Operators.
- ◆ Guests.

The default groups are used to give privileges to groups or users. The Administrators and Power Users groups have been mentioned briefly in this section. The Users group provides an account with a user status and basic control privileges. One of the key features provided by the Users group is the ability for a user to manage groups he or she has created. A user can perform any management tasks for a group that he or she created. Users do not have access to other groups. The personal user profile (preferences) is also triggered by placing a user account in the Users group. A user that is a member of the Users group has his or her preferences saved and restored each time the user logs in to or out of the workstation.

The Guests group is used to allow a user to access minimum resources on a workstation. The Backup Operators group identifies its members as having the ability to back up files on the workstation. The Backup Operators group is a nice feature because it allows a user to back up and restore files but does not necessarily give the user access to the files.

NT has four other default groups that do not have members. These groups are used to define how the user uses the workstation. The groups are:

- ◆ Interactive Users.
- ◆ Network Users.
- ◆ Everyone.
- ◆ Creator/Owner.

The Interactive Users group identifies users who log on to the workstation interactively. NT accounts can be used for purposes other than interactive access, such as providing application programs with a certain access privilege. The Network Users group contains all users who access the workstation over the network. Every interactive and network user is a member of the Everyone group. A user who creates a file, directory, or print job is a member of the Creator/Owner group for that object. This includes a user that takes ownership of an object.

Groups are created and managed with User Manager. The New Local Group dialog is used to create a new group. To create a new local group, select New Local Group from the User Menu. Simply enter the group name and description, and then click OK. You can add users to the new group when you create it by first selecting the users and then selecting New Local Group. See the discussion on Groups in Chapter 9 for the steps required to create and manage groups.

Login Scripts

Login scripts are a tool that most network managers use to automate tasks when a user logs in to a workstation. Login scripts are executed every time a user logs in. They are very much like AUTOEXEC.BAT files on PCs, which are executed whenever a PC boots, except that a login script executes each time a user logs in. NT supports login scripts for all users. NT login scripts can be either batch files (.BAT or .CMD) or executable files (EXE). Executable files can be either character-based or Windows programs.

The type of tasks performed by a login script will vary from system to system. Tasks may be as simple as checking for electronic mail messages or may be complex operations such as starting applications or connecting to remote network resources.

Login scripts can be activated in two ways. The first and most common is to specify the login script in User Manager for a particular user. The second method is to place a reference to the login script program in the Startup group for the user. The Startup group executes all programs in the group every time a user logs in. This is because NT stores personal program manager groups by user.

You may be wondering how to manage login scripts because of the flexibility that NT offers. Should you use batch files, executable programs, or a special batch language? How should the programs be started? The type of login scripts that you use and the manner in which they are executed will depend on your installation. Let's review some guidelines on the proper use of login scripts.

Before we start this discussion, let's consider the difference between a true login script and programs that are placed in the Startup group. A true login script is one created by a system manager or system owner that he or she wishes to execute each time a particular user logs in to the system. Programs placed in the Startup group are usually programs that a user wishes to execute when he or she logs in. On a standalone computer, there is little difference between the two. It may be easier to place the commands in the Startup group, because they will be easier to access. Programs in the Startup group also have the advantage of being easily accessible after the user logs in. All references to login scripts in this chapter refer to true login scripts specified in User Manager.

The Startup group adds a lot of flexibility, because it does basically the same thing as a login script, but it can be modified by the user and is executed separately from the login script. If a user creates a problem with the Startup group, it will usually affect only programs the user has entered in the group and not facilities the system manager has established.

Login scripts should be executed by placing the program name in the user profile in the User Manager Profile dialog. A login script is a program defined by the system manager to execute specific things for a user when the user logs in. Users should not have access to modify login scripts, because doing so could create problems for the user. Imagine what would happen if you had a network of 100 or more PCs and users could change their own login scripts.

A login script can be either a batch program or an executable program. The major difference between batch programs and executable programs is the speed of execution and the inaccessibility of the source for executable programs. Batch programs always run slower than executable programs, because they are executed by interpreting each line as they run. Executable programs are either machine language programs or highly compact files that execute very quickly.

Batch programs have a distinct advantage: They can be modified very quickly and do not require compiling before they can be executed. This ease of modification can be a drawback, because it can lead to many versions of the same program if you use somewhat standard login scripts for different users. Executable programs are a little more difficult to modify, because they must be compiled before execution. This usually leads to a more controlled environment with fewer versions of the same program.

User Manager is used to specify a login script for a user. The User Profile dialog contains a field for the login script name. The name of the file should be entered here. Login scripts must be stored in the NT root (\WINNT) directory. WINNT is the default name for the NT root directory.

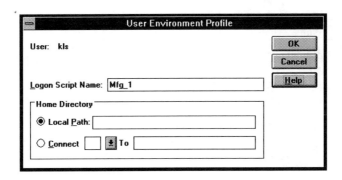

User Manager - User Profile Dialog

Startup group programs can also be batch or executable programs. The Startup group also makes the task of installing a program very easy. Because it uses Windows drag-and-drop facilities, you can place a program in the Startup group by dragging a program name from File Manager or dragging a program icon from another group. A program can also be placed in the Startup group by using the File Menu and selecting the New Option.

Managing System Configurations

The Windows Control Panel is one of those time-honored utilities that has been around for a long time. It has also undergone a number of changes and enhancements as Windows has evolved and been improved over the years. Windows V3.x added additional flexibility to Control Panel by allowing it to dynamically load new control managers to match the flexibility of a particular machine. Adding a new sound card or the hardware components will probably add or enable certain Control Panel features that were previously turned off.

Windows NT has built on top of the V3.x Control Manager foundation by adding features for managing numerous NT components. In addition to the standard features, NT adds management features for several system components, including system functions, the NT server, services, devices, and uninterruptible power supplies (UPS). Other utilities have been modified to work with NT's features.

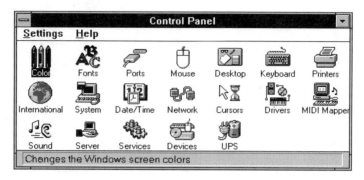

Control Panel

Many Control Panel functions in NT apply only to a particular user's preferences, while others affect the entire NT system. As discussed in Chapter 5, Windows NT stores a user's preferences in the system Registry, instead of in an .INI, as does Windows V3.1. You should think of a user's preference as anything that affects the appearance of the system, but not its function. In other words, desktop color settings or the appearance of a user's Program Manager group would be considered a preference and would probably be different for each user that has an account on the NT workstation.

Special care should be used whenever you change an option that could affect other users. For instance, changing the Desktop colors normally affects only a single user. Deleting a color scheme deletes the actual settings from the machine, making it unavailable to all users.

Date and Time

The Date/Time applet in Control Panel has a nice feature that supports daylight-saving time. Select your time zone, and then check the Automatically Adjust box; you will not have to reset the time twice each year in the spring and fall.

Data/Time Dialog

System

The System applet is used to configure certain system components of NT, including environment variables and NT's boot configuration.

NT environment variables are separated into two categories: system variables and user variables. Using the System applet to change environment variables works almost exactly like the Tools/Options/Win.ini feature in Word for Windows. The settings shown in the User Environment Variables section dialog will be for the user that is currently logged in. The username will be displayed in the title for the user environment variables.

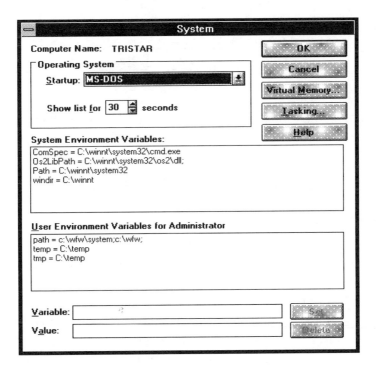

System Applet

The Operating System box allows you to configure the boot parameters for your system. The Startup list box will list all operating systems that are on your system and have been configured with FlexBoot. The information is stored in the BOOT.INI file in the root directory of your system for Intel systems.

Selecting an entry from the list will cause that option to be the default operating system when the computer boots. The Show List For box contains the number of seconds the system will wait before starting the default operating system. The default value is 30 seconds.

The Tasking button allows you to set the multitasking priorities of the workstation. These types of applications are programs that interact with the user and are not minimized. Background applications are programs that are minimized or batch programs that do not interact with the user.

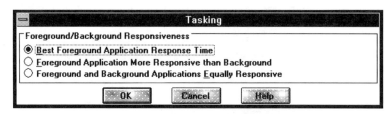

Tasking Dialog

The first button on the dialog will set NT for the best possible performance for applications that are running in the foreground. The second button makes background tasks more responsive, but foreground tasks are still more responsive than the background tasks. The last button makes foreground and background tasks equally responsive.

Environment Variables

NT extends the use of environment variables that we have become accustomed to in MS-DOS, as discussed in Chapter 5. Environment variables can be created or changed by a program at the command prompt with the SET command or from Control Panel using the System applet.

Environment variables are useful for storing information that is passed from one program to another or that should be available to programs for an extended period of time. NT adds to the functionality of DOS by using three different classes of environment variables: system, AUTOEXEC, and user. System variables are restricted for use by NT and cannot be changed. The other two classes are very useful for NT programs and utilities.

Like many things that happen within NT, user variables are linked to a specific user and are created when the user logs in and destroyed when the user logs out. The system variables are set when NT boots, similar to what happens in an AUTOEXEC.BAT file for a DOS-based system.

The NT PATH Variable

NT uses the PATH variable for its search path just as DOS does. NT handles the path in a different manner than DOS, because it builds the path for each user when he or she logs in.

NT sets the default path when it boots. The first item in the path will always be \WINNT\SYSTEM32; WINNT is the NT root directory. User and application directories always follow the default part of the path. If you look in the System applet in Control Panel, you will notice that PATH shows up as an NT system variable with the value of \WINNT\SYSTEM32. You can also set the path as a user variable, causing NT to append this value to its default path. The next figure shows the System applet with the path set both in the System box and the User box.

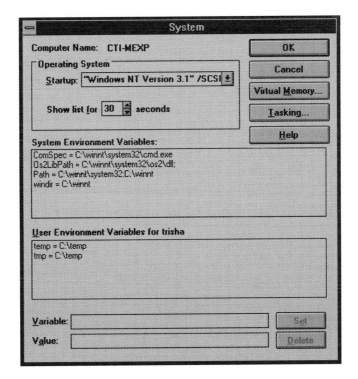

System Applet with PATH Settings

NT takes the two settings for the path and concatenates them resulting in a path like this:

```
C:\WINNT\SYSTEM32;C:\WFW\SYSTEM;C:\WFW;
```

You can also modify the path to some extent at the command prompt. The %PATH% variable can be used at the command prompt as well as in batch files. The following command will add C:\DOC to the end of the path:

```
C:\>PATH = %PATH% + C:\DOC;
```

The path variable also gets set in the AUTOEXEC.BAT file. This occurs when a user logs in to an NT system. The System applet does not reflect changes made to the path variable in the AUTOEXEC.BAT file.

Adding a Disk Drive

Adding a disk drive to an NT system is a fairly straightforward task. The process is slightly less intimidating than adding a disk to a DOS system because of NT's easy-to-use Disk Administrator program. However, Disk Administrator does not alleviate hassles with some hardware platforms. Some systems, such as PCs, were originally designed to have only one or two hard disks, while others were designed to be extensible.

NT supports many disk systems because of the different types of hardware on which it runs. Most RISC systems and many PCs will use SCSI drives, while PCs may also use other drives, such as IDE or MFM. Other platforms may use other disks such as the DSSI systems from Digital that run on DEC midrange platforms.

SCSI drives are probably the easiest drives to configure, as long as your system has a SCSI adapter installed. SCSI devices are numbered from zero to seven, allowing up to six devices on the same adapter; the SCSI controller counts as one device. Most systems will also support more than one controller, providing a growth path for lots of storage.

You may run into problems with SCSI drives on PC systems when you add SCSI adapters to your system. Most SCSI adapters map into the same upper memory range that is used by your network card. These adapters can cause problems when you try to squeeze two or three adapters that each want 16 to 32 KB of memory and a network adapter that needs 32 to 64 KB of memory into the same upper memory area. This problem is specific to Intel PCs because of its architecture. Most RISC systems come with a built-in SCSI adapter and provide support for adding drives.

Just a few hints for before you go off and begin adding drives. Determine what type of drives your system has and the configuration of the drives, such as jumper settings.

Also find out whether your system can support more drives. Does it have enough power cables? How about the wattage rating on the power supply? Does the disk controller support more drives? SCSI systems support up to seven drives on one controller, while IDE controllers can handle only two drives. You should also check the documentation for the controller and drives to determine any master/slave relationships for non-SCSI systems.

After you have braved the hardware challenges and the new drive is at home in your system, you can restart the machine. Log in as Administrator and run Disk Administrator. Disk Administrator will be very polite, informing you that you have added drives since the last time that Disk Administrator was run and that its files are going to be updated. Once the update is complete, which should only take a few seconds, you should see a screen similar to the one below.

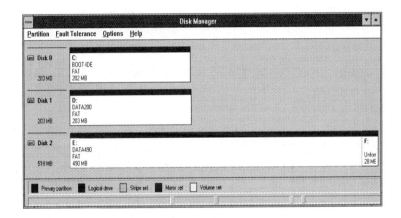

Disk Administrator

This graphic shows three drives on this NT system with free space on the F: drive. If you have just added a drive, Disk Administrator will display the total drive as raw. There are two steps to complete the installation of your drive. The first step is to select (click) the disk area that you wish to set up and select Partition Disk from the Partition menu. Enter the drive letter and select how much space NT should use for the new partition. Once you have completed this step, Disk Administrator will tell you that it must restart.

Once NT is back up, log in as Administrator and start the command prompt. The last step is to format the drive before it can be used. We will stray from the friendly interface of Disk Administrator to the old familiar DOS Format command. This is the same old Format that has been around for many years, except that it is now a 32-bit program and has a new switch or two. The only switch of concern at this point is the FS (File System) switch that we will use to tell NT which file system to use. The options for the file system option are:

Option	Description
FAT	The FAT option formats the drive for the DOS file system.
HPFS	HPFS formats the disk for an OS/2-style file system.
NTFS	The NTFS option prepares a drive for the new NTFS file system.

The command syntax to prepare the drive with format is:

```
C:\> FORMAT F: /FS:NTFS
```

You will get the standard warning that NT is going to blow away all the files on your disk. Make sure this is your new disk before answering yes. If there is any doubt, answer no and restart the command.

After format finishes, your new disk should be ready to use. I usually like to perform a quick test by copying a file or two to the disk and then doing a directory on the drive. If everything goes OK, you are in business.

One last note on adding disks to an NT system. NT can support multiple file systems on the same drive. Each file system must be in its own partition. Simply create multiple partitions with Disk Administrator and then format each partition for the appropriate file system. NT also provides the Convert command to move old file systems (FAT) to NTFS. Convert provides a nice growth path by allowing you to use a FAT file system until all your applications become NTFS-aware and then convert the file system to NTFS with one command.

Upgrading or Adding an NTFS Partition

The Convert command is used to upgrade a FAT or HPFS partition to NTFS if it was not upgraded during the installation process. The format for Convert is:

```
C:\>CONVERT /FS:NTFS D:
```

This command converts the D: drive to an NTFS partition.

Convert only works on FAT or HPFS partitions and converts them to NTFS. It will not convert an NTFS partition back to HPFS or FAT.

Removing DOS

You can remove DOS or any other operating system entirely from your machine once NT is installed. The steps will vary depending on your hardware and operating system. Intel machines can use the following procedure:

1. Disable the multiboot option by clearing the other systems from the operating system list. Use the System applet in Control Panel for this task.

2. Delete the DOS files from your disk. These files usually consist of COMMAND.COM and all the files in your DOS directory.

3. Copy CONFIG.NT to CONFIG.SYS.

4. Copy AUTOEXEC.NT to AUTOEXEC.BAT.

5. Run CONVERT.EXE to convert your FAT file system to NTFS. This step is optional.

Home Directory

The term Home Directory applies to the current drive and directory after a user logs in. The Home Directory is the place where a user will keep his or her personal files and can feel certain that the files cannot be accessed by others.

NT uses the \USERS\DEFAULT directory as the user's login directory, unless you choose another path for the directory in the Profile dialog when the user account is created or modified.

Replicator Service

The Replicator is designed to simplify the task of keeping files in sync on a network. The replicator will automatically copy files across the network at specific intervals. This is another of those handy little features that makes the Advanced Server worth looking at if you manage a sizable network. The Replicator Service on a standard NT system can import files only from an NT Advanced Server system. You must run NT Advanced Server to both export and import files.

Resource Management

System Backup

Backup procedures and programs are one of the most important parts of a system management plan. Backup procedures will not seem very important until your system crashes a disk or has important data destroyed in some other manner. Losing data is a major inconvenience for a system that is used at home for letters and games. Losing data on a system used in business can be disastrous, possibly even causing the failure of the business.

NT provides a number of features for managing the backup chores of your system or network. The most visible feature is the Backup program in the Administrative group. Backup is a powerful utility that is a far cry from the original Backup program shipped with MS-DOS. Backup is an important and easy-to-use tool that is well-documented in the NT manuals. Instead of focusing on the Backup program, let's look at the underlying features that NT provides for backup chores.

Backup programs must have access to the files that they will backup. A Backup program is actually just copying files from one disk to another or to a tape drive. Most systems that have built-in security require that users performing backup tasks be given access to the files they back up. This can be a daunting task in a secure environment because of the requirements for security.

NT allows all users to back up files they own, either because they created them or because they took ownership of them. The Backup group is provided to allow a user to back up files and/or system files that the user does not own. A user in the Backup group can back up and restore the entire system, including NT system files.

Any drive connected to an NT workstation is automatically shared as an Administrative share. An Administrative share can be connected to only by users in the Administrative group or Backup group. This removes the hassles of establishing some method of access that gives backup operators permission to access files but protects the system from security violations. Network backup routines can connect to all Administrative shares on the network and perform the necessary backup chores.

The next question is, what do we back up? Performing a full backup every day is a great idea but requires a tremendous amount of storage space on the backup media. Most system managers perform a data backup or some type of modified backup. The most important thing when performing a limited backup is to find a method for easily determining which files should be backed up.

One of the easiest methods of determining which files to back up is to construct your directory structure to provide a means of automatically selecting files. NT provides the basis of this structure during installation. The default parent directory for all user accounts is the \USERS directory. Unless you specify another directory, NT will place your user accounts under this directory. This simplifies the backup tasks, because you can specify that your backup program copy all files and subdirectories under the USERS directory. This will back up all user data that is kept under the \USERS directory.

You should also establish a common parent directory for all other data directories. This will typically include shared directories and directories for database or similar files. This can be accomplished by placing these directories under the USERS directory or creating another parent directory (such as \DATA). With this structure you can back up two directory trees and secure all your user data. The same structure can be repeated if you have data on multiple drives.

Once all the user data and shared files are taken care of, we are done, right? Wrong! The last thing to back up on a routine basis is the NT database in the \WINNT\SYSTEM32\CONFIG directory and any other system files that frequently change. CONFIG.*, AUTOEXEC.*, and all *.INI files are good candidates. This should also include application-specific files such as the *.DOT files that Word for Windows uses for templates. Make sure your backup routine also includes these files in its daily routine.

System and application files should also be backed up on some regular basis, unless you don't mind reinstalling multiple programs when your system loses a disk. Some programs may stuff files, such as Microsoft Word for Windows template files, in their default directory. Many of these idiosyncrasies will be around for a long time as we transition from DOS to NT.

Protecting against Power Problems

A UPS is a vital component for any system that is used regularly for business or that contains valuable documents. This includes any machine that is used as a LAN server, whether or not the system is used in a server-only or a peer-to-peer NT network.

The UPS service can send and receive messages to a UPS connected to the NT system. These messages include the UPS signal to NT that power has failed, a message from the UPS to NT indicating that the battery is getting low, and a message from NT to the UPS indicating that it is OK for the UPS to shut down.

The most critical message is the one from the UPS to NT indicating that power has failed. The UPS applet has a field for the length of battery life (Expected Battery Life) for recording the length of time, in minutes, that the battery is expected to support NT when power fails. When power fails, NT can monitor the length of time the battery is used and shut down accordingly.

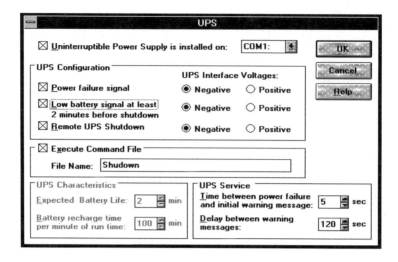

UPS Applet

If the UPS provides more sophisticated features such as notifying NT when the battery is low, NT will use this information, because it is more accurate. The data carrier detected (DCD) serial line is used to signal NT that there are 2 minutes of power left in the UPS. Select this option in the UPS applet by selecting Low Battery Signal at least 2 Minutes before Shutdown.

The Execute Command File option in the UPS dialog will cause the specified program to be executed when the UPS is 2 minutes from shutting down. Make sure that the program is a short one and does not take longer than 2 minutes!

NT can also send a message to the UPS notifying it to shut down. The DTR signal is used by NT to send a signal to the UPS to shut itself down. Select this option by choosing Remote UPS Shutdown.

POWERING DOWN AN NT SYSTEM

Caution: You should always use the Shutdown option on the File menu in Program Manager to shut down your NT system. NT must be properly shut down to allow it to properly flush its buffers and memory to disk. Simply powering down the system without using Shutdown may cause a loss of data.

NTFS is designed to be very robust and may not have problems if it is shut down in the middle of an operation. However, it is still good practice to properly shut down all NT systems, because you do not know what processes and actions are running on the system.

INSTALLATION

Installing NT should be a simple task for most users. This discussion focuses briefly on the standard NT installation procedures. You should consult your NT documentation for the specific type of machine you are using and also review your machine's documentation regarding NT.

As of this writing, NT does not support compressed drives. This means that if you are using Stacker, DoubleSpace, or any other stacking mechanism for a drive, you must uncompress the drive before installing NT. If you do not, you will not be able to access the files on the stacked drive from NT. This situation will change, because I am sure that third-party vendors will bring compression technology to NT and Microsoft will add compression at some time. Check the NT documentation for your version of NT to determine whether it supports stacked drives before proceeding with installation. You could also contact STAC Electronics and other vendors of compression technologies.

Prerequisites

If you are installing NT on a pre-1993 RISC machine, you should call your vendor's support staff before beginning the installation process. Tell them that you are going to use NT and ask what specific steps should be taken to perform the installation on your hardware. You should also ask them if there are any hardware upgrades that must be performed before NT is installed.

If your system will be used on a network, read Chapter 4 and pay close attention to the discussions on installing network adapters and software, and setting the computer and workgroup names.

You will also need the names and models of any printers that are attached to your system. You can add printer drivers after NT is installed if you prefer to wait.

NT Installation Methods

NT offers several methods of installation that will simplify the process. The installation methods all use the familiar Setup program introduced with Windows V3.1 and now used by all versions of Windows and most Windows application programs.

The Unsupported CD-ROM and Network methods use a slight variation of Setup, because the installation process must be started from DOS. NT provides a program called WINNT that will begin the installation process before loading Setup. In both cases, WINNT copies all the NT files to the hard disk of the machine. After the files are copied, the machine is rebooted, and Setup takes over to finish the installation.

Intel Systems can use the following methods for installing NT:

◆ Floppy disk.

◆ SCSI CD-ROM drives.

◆ Unsupported CD-ROM drives.

◆ Network.

◆ Profile.

RISC systems must the CD-ROM installation process.

The standard NT software package supports all the methods mentioned except for the Profile method. The Profile method is supported by the NT Resource Kit, which is available from Microsoft.

The Floppy and CD-ROM methods can be used on standalone PCs or PCs that are attached to a network. The Network and Profile methods are used for network installations only.

NT will request that a blank diskette be labeled as an Emergency disk during the installation process. NT will prompt you to insert the disk at the appropriate time and will copy the Registry database to the floppy. This disk is very important, because it will be needed if there is a major problem with the machine. The Emergency disk is specific to a particular machine and cannot be used on any other machine. Also note that the Emergency disk must be placed in drive A. No other drive will work.

Microsoft provides several suggestions to keep in mind when installing NT:

◆ When the Setup process asks you to reboot the machine, read the message on the screen. Setup will tell you whether you should remove the diskette or leave it in the drive. If you do not heed this message, you may have to start over.

◆ Installation of NT Advanced Server requires that a network card be installed before the installation process starts.

◆ You should plan a minimum of 1 hour for the installation process on your first machine.

◆ When you are using the Network method, start the process by entering C:\>WINNT -X. This will cause Setup to not build another emergency disk.

TUNING AN NT SYSTEM

This section takes a brief look at tuning an NT system. Because NT is a new system and has not been used in large systems, this discussion will focus on known problem areas that will affect NT's performance. Stay tuned to the magazines and future publications for more information about turning NT in large and complex environments.

Page Files - More Memory

NT uses a feature called virtual memory to extend the available memory of your system by using a special area on your hard disk to act as additional memory. NT will move (swap) programs from real memory to the virtual memory file (called a "page" or "swap" file) when it needs to access more memory. The applications that are swapped out of memory will be the least-used programs that are currently in memory. NT will automatically retrieve the program from the virtual memory file when it is accessed again, either by a user or another process. Virtual memory has been around for a long time and should be familiar to Windows V3.x users.

The virtual memory page file is called PAGEFILE.SYS and is a hidden file in the system partition. This file can't be deleted when running NT. The recommended size is the RAM size of your system plus 12 MB, with a minimum size of 20 MB. The Control Panel is used to set up virtual memory.

The Windows NT documentation suggests creating multiple page files — a maximum of 16 — if you have more than one fixed disk. Having separate page files on different disks may improve performance by spreading the I/O for the page files across the different disks. The amount of performance improvement will depend on the type and speed of the disks and the type of controller used. Controllers that can simultaneously access two disks will provide a distinct advantage over ones that can access only one disk at a time.

The following figure shows the Virtual Memory dialog from the System applet.

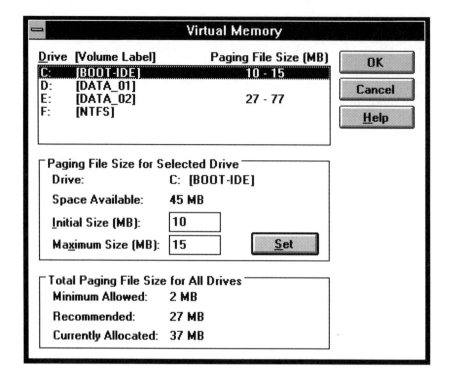

Virtual Memory Dialog

This example has two page files. The first page file is a minimum of 10 MB and a maximum 15 MB and is located on the C: drive. The disk in this case a 202-MB IDE drive on a fast local bus IDE controller. The second page file is 27 MB and is located on a SCSI disk that is attached to a fast local bus SCSI adapter. NT supports up to 16 page files.

NT can maximize the throughput of your system with this type of configuration by splitting the use of the page files across both disk drives. Because the drives use different controllers, the system will not spend much time waiting on a controller.

You can remove a page file by setting both the initial size and maximum size to 0 and clicking OK. Make sure you have selected the correct drive before you change the settings.

Disk Fragmentation
Another important note from the documentation concerns the use of a disk defragmentor. As data is written and deleted from a disk drive over time, gaps of free

space are created across the drive. This fragmented area becomes larger and larger as a drive is used over time.

The problem is compounded when new data is written to a fragmented area, because a single file may be spread over two or more sections of disk. This occurs when there is no one area big enough to hold the file.

A badly fragmented disk will have files that are spread all over the disk and has very little contiguous free space. A defragmentor simply rearranges the disk, placing each file in a contiguous area and making all free space contiguous. Running this type of utility frequently will drastically improve the performance of your system. Defragmentors should be run before any major change that affects your disk system, such as changing the paging files or adding new applications.

Disk Errors

NT performs a disk check at system startup on each drive that it has marked "dirty." Checking disk systems during the startup process and correcting comes from NT's UNIX and OpenVMS heritage. These systems have had disk error checking during the boot process for many years. NTFS is also less likely to have problems than FAT or HPFS because it was designed for fault tolerance from the ground up.

CHKDSK /F can be run from the Command prompt after startup for all drive, except the NT system partition. This is because CHKDSK cannot lock the entire system drive before performing its analysis and corrections.

Monitoring System and Application Events

One of the most difficult tasks in managing any system is collecting performance and event data over time and monitoring the changes. This also requires establishing a set of baseline data to which new events are compared. Event Viewer and other tools such as Excel, Visual Basic, and Winbatch provide tools for simplifying the collection and analysis of event and performance data. The next section provides an example of how data can be extracted from Event logs and analyzed in Excel.

Performance Monitor and Event Viewer can monitor an astonishing number of events that occur within an NT system and in some cases other systems. Performance Monitor is used to track the performance of your system and maintains counters that record almost every aspect of your system. Event Viewer is used to track auditing logs and events that are recorded by system and application programs.

Performance Monitor provides a number of tricks and tools for managing a typical system. For instance, you can configure a chart with the counters that are important for one type of study and save the chart by name for use later. You can also have the performance of certain counters tracked over time and the data stored in a log file.

The log file can then be reviewed in Performance Monitor. A number of other tools are also provided, including the ability to set Alerts that will perform some action when the Alert is triggered.

Event Viewer can be used to monitor and manage information on system and application events. Event Viewer provides a number of options for selecting event logs and filtering the event information. Another nice feature is the ability to save a log file in comma-delimited format for use by other applications.

Because Event Viewer and Performance Monitor are such powerful tools, each has its own chapter following this chapter. You should review these chapters for more information about these products.

CHOOSING A HARDWARE PLATFORM FOR NT

NT is the most exciting operating environment to come along in a long time because it supports many hardware platforms while maintaining software compatibility. Hardware requirements vary from user to user, depending on the user's needs and the types of software he or she is running. Graphics, factory floor, and other CPU-intensive programs require all the horsepower available, while simple word processing applications may use a lower power workstation.

This difference in hardware requirements has traditionally been a dilemma for systems managers, making it difficult or even impossible to standardize on hardware platforms and operating systems. NT solves this dilemma by running on virtually any hardware platform available and still running the same software. The flexibility of NT also provides a growth for applications to be developed on a low-cost system and easily ported to a more powerful processor and vice versa.

The Windows World Trade Show in May 1993 provided a glimpse of the future with a number of new systems designed specifically for NT. The following benchmark information was recorded from a demonstration at Digital's booth:

Task/System	Alpha AXP	Intel 486/66
Electronic CAD	1:12	3:15
Video Clip	0:32	2:15

The tasks consisted of the following:

◆ Electronic CAD simulation displaying a complex circuit layout.

◆ A 34-second video clip of a movie segment.

These two tasks demonstrate the performance capabilities of the Alpha AXP-based machines. The Alpha AXP PC used in the demo was actually a preproduction unit. Notice that the electronic CAD task was performed in almost one-third the time, while the video clip ran in less than one-sixth the time.

Systems using the Alpha AXP chip, the new MIPS Technologies chips, and the Intergraph Clipper chips will bring unheard-of performance levels to the user population.

Intel-Based PCs

NT will run on workstations powered by high-end Intel processors. Microsoft suggests that a PC have a minimum of 8 MB of memory, 65 MB of free disk space, and a 386/25 or higher processor. I would strongly suggest using a 486/33 as the minimum platform for NT, 12 MB of RAM, and 70 to 75 MB of free disk space. The disk figures include room for a 15-MB page file on the minimum system and a 20- to 25-MB page file on the recommended system.

A system running NT Advanced Server should have a minimum of 12 MB (16 MB suggested), 70 MB of free disk (75 MB suggested), and a 486/33 processor.

PCs based on the new Intel Pentium processor are well-suited to NT. These machines will outperform the fastest 486 PCs. As the Pentium machines mature, they should provide even more performance gains. The Pentium should also be well-suited for multiprocessor PCs designed specially for NT.

Many vendors are now offering Intel platforms designed from the ground up to run Windows, both NT only and NT/Windows V3.1 versions. Vendors of these systems include traditional PC vendors plus many vendors that formerly produced only UNIX systems. The standard configuration for these machines usually has a lot of disk (100 to 200 MB), a lot of memory (8 to 16 MB), and a local bus for video and possibly other services. These PCs should continue to improve and add new features as we move from DOS-compatible PCs to a true Windows compatibles that are optimized for running Windows.

RISC

NT will also run on a wide variety of RISC processors currently on the market. One of the newest entries to the RISC field is the Alpha AXP RISC platform from Digital, which offers the promise of a processor for the future and fantastic performance for now. The Alpha AXP architecture is one of the most exciting things to hit the computer scene in a long time. The initial chips are running at clock speeds of 100 to 200 MHz. This processor powers systems ranging from desktop systems to mainframes more powerful than anything on the planet. There are also rumors of laptops and other possible uses for Alpha AXP.

Other promising platforms are MIPS R4000-based systems and HP's Precision Architecture line. R4000-based systems are manufactured by a number of vendors and provide very good performance for NT. The HP Precision Architecture is also a popular and powerful system and is backed by the super reputation of HP, one of the finest hardware companies in the world. Support for other processors is in the works, including the Sun Sparcstation and IBM's RISC machines.

RISC processors offer several features that make them attractive for NT platforms. Because of its minicomputer heritage, a typical RISC-based workstation will offer more robust and reliable options than a typical Intel-based workstation. These services include fast and reliable disk drives (including disk arrays and disk farms), large-capacity backup devices (tape storage units), CD-ROM servers, optical jukeboxes, special 2-D and 3-D graphics boards, and many other features. The networking products for typical RISC workstations are also very robust, providing a wide variety of standard options for a complex LAN or WAN. The biggest change in running NT on a RISC processor noticed by most users is the vast performance improvement over older Intel platforms.

RISC vendors usually have their own or a third-party service organization for maintaining your equipment, including telephone support and onsite service. This is an ideal situation for companies that have minicomputer systems or other large systems that are under a service contract, because the vendor can service all equipment in the organization. The customer support and field service personnel for RISC vendors are also much more knowledgeable about networks and other high-end problems than their PC counterparts.

Hardware Features for Nearly All Machines

The following list includes a number of features that are useful for most systems running NT. These features will improve the disk and graphics performance of your NT system, two of the most important areas for NT. Newer systems will be introduced in the near future that will have other bus and graphics structures that will outperform the ones listed. Stay in touch with the reviews published by the most popular magazines for the latest news on hardware improvements.

- Fast I/O bus (VESA or other).
- Multiple fast disk drives.

◆ High-speed graphics processor with NT drivers.

◆ 16 MB or more system memory.

For Intel PCs, contact the system vendor and make certain that the system will support more than 16 MB. Some systems have problems running NT when more than 16 MB is installed.

CHAPTER 7

Performance Monitor

PERFORMANCE MONITOR OVERVIEW

Performance Monitor is a powerful tool for tracking problems, diagnosing system and network problems, and monitoring the status of your system. The number of events that this tool can monitor and its ease of use are truly outstanding. Performance Monitor builds on NT's open architecture, allowing third-party products to plug into these monitoring tools. Lets take a peek at a few features and see how to use this tool on your system.

Performance Monitor is a super tool for viewing information about the status of your system or other NT systems on a network. This includes the current operation of the system in real-time or information saved over time. Events can be for the system running Performance Monitor or for any number of other NT systems on your network.

User Interface

Saving Session Settings

Performance Monitor can store the settings for a session, allowing you to retrieve the configuration for use at a later time. The default settings file is _DEFAULT.xxx. The extension (xxx) will be PMC (Chart), PMA (Alert), PML (Log), or PMR (Report). You can save settings for a single window by selecting File/Save Settings in that window.

Settings for all windows can be saved by selecting File/Save Workspace. The term *workspace* is used to define the configuration of a Performance Monitor session and contains the configuration of all windows and settings.

Be careful when you change settings on a window or workspace and click File/Save. Remember that File/Save will overwrite the default settings, or, if you have opened a settings file, it will update the settings to the current ones. If you want to save the default settings and your new settings, choose File/Save As. Clicking File/Save Workspace will always present you with the Save dialog, which allows you to save to the current or different file.

Configuring Display Features

The Options menu allows you to toggle on or off the display of the Menu and title bar, toolbar, and status bar, providing a clear view of the windows. Double-clicking in a blank spot of the display area will toggle the display of the menu bar and toolbar on and off, while pressing Ctrl-S will toggle the status bar on and off.

An important option for troubleshooting your system is provided by the Windows API Always on Top function. This function will keep the Program Monitor window on top of all other windows even when it doesn't have the focus. Always on Top is useful when you need to continually monitor your system and continue working at the same time. This is especially useful on systems that have 1,024- x 768-pixel or larger displays in which you can stick Performance Monitor in a small corner of the display and keep working. This option is toggled on and off by setting the Always on Top option on the Options menu.

The Performance Monitor Toolbar

Performance Monitor uses a standard toolbar at the top of the screen. This toolbar allows you to quickly select a function with one click of the mouse. The toolbar options are shown below.

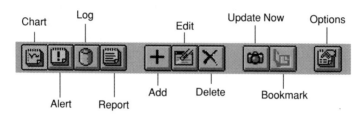

The buttons are defined in the following table.

Button	Description
Chart	Displays the Chart window.
Alert	Displays the Alert window.
Log	Displays the Log window.
Report	Displays the Report window.
Add	Displays the Add dialog for the current window, allowing you to add items. The dialog will vary for each window.
Edit	Displays the Edit dialog for the currently selected item, allowing you to change the options for the object.
Delete	Deletes the current item from the window.
Update Now	Performs an instant update of the counters. The shortcut is F5.
Bookmark	Inserts a bookmark at the current location.
Options	Displays the options dialog for the current window.

You can select an options work by clicking on the toolbar button. The Details button requires that you select an item in a window before clicking on Details.

Performance Monitor Windows

Performance Monitor can display information in four formats: Chart, Alert, Log, and Report. Each format has a particular use and is flexible in the way it displays information. Performance Monitor uses individual windows for its displays, allowing you to configure Performance Monitor with one window for each type of display, or different views of the same window. The following discussion provides a brief overview of each type of display and features common to all windows.

Each window shares the menu bar, status bar, log symbol (if currently logging), and toolbar. You will notice that the menu options change with the type of window displayed.

The log symbol will be displayed in the status bar of each window when logging is enabled. The log symbol will display the continually changing size of the log file.

Log Symbol

You can clear a window at any time by selecting Edit/Clear Display. This will clear the data from the window but does not delete any items from the display.

Chart Window

The Chart window displays performance data in graphical chart format. The charts are very flexible and allow you to display only the information required for a particular task. There are a number of output options under the File menu for printing charts or exporting data to other file formats.

The Chart window can display either line graphs or histograms. Line graphs are most useful for data tracked over time. Histograms are useful for looking at snapshots as things occur and for observing many simultaneous items.

You can highlight a line in the chart window by clicking on the line's description in the legend. This will turn the chart line white. Chart highlighting is turned on and off by pressing Ctrl-H

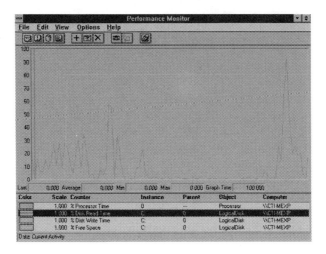

Chart Window

The Chart Options dialog allows you to select several aspects of the chart's appearance. These settings include check boxes to turn on or off the display of the Legend, Vertical Labels, Vertical Grid, Horizontal Grid, and Value Bar. Selecting a check box turns the option on, while unchecking the box hides the option.

You can also change the maximum value for the vertical scale. The Time Interval specifies how often the display is automatically updated. The Group box has buttons for toggling between a Graph (default) or Histogram. The Chart Options dialog is shown below.

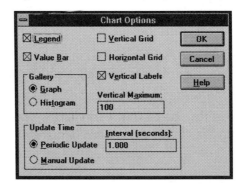

Chart Options Dialog

This dialog also allows you to select either a Graph or Histogram display for the Chart window. The two versions are shown below.

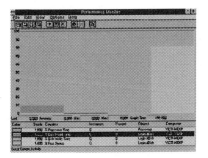 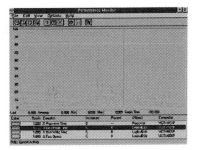

Types of Chart Displays: Graph and Histogram

The Graph display will probably be the most frequently used format, because it provides an easy-to-read display for trends and quickly highlights counters with high values. It is also great for analyzing multiple counters at the same time and looking for a correlation.

Alert Window

The Alert window displays a list of objects that have exceeded alert values. Each time an alert criterion is met, a new recording for that item is logged in the Alert window. Alerts can be added to perform actions such as notification of a user when an alert occurs. Performance Monitor can also run a program once or each time the counter drops below a certain value. These options are extremely powerful for managing your system. They can be used to alert the administrator when events occur or even run programs that take corrective action when certain levels are reached.

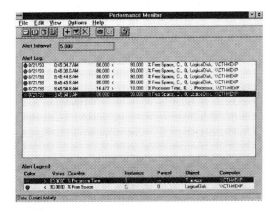

Alert Window

The Alert Options dialog is shown in the next figure. This dialog allows you to set several parameters that affect alerts and how alerts are treated.

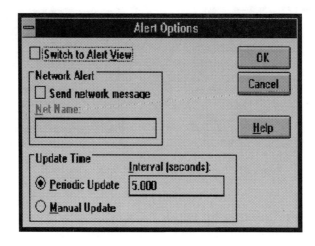

Alert Options Dialog

The Switch to Alert View option tells Performance Monitor to automatically switch to the Alert view when an alert occurs. If you have a lot of items selected for alerts or have set the alert parameters so that your system receives a high number of alerts, you may want to turn this option off to prevent Performance Monitor from constantly switching to the Alert view.

The Network Alert check box allows Performance Monitor to send a message to another workstation when an alert occurs. This option should be set with the same care that is used for the Switch to Alert View, or you will bombard someone with alerts and add a lot of traffic to your network. If you use this option, you should enter the destination computer name for alert messages in the Net Name field. The destination computer must be running the Messenger service to receive alert messages.

The Update Time field works the same way as the Update Time fields in the other Performance Monitor options. The two buttons determine whether Alerts are automatically checked (the time value specifies how often Alerts are checked) or whether you must manually tell Performance Monitor when to check for alerts.

Log Window
The Log window displays information about the currently active log file. The information includes the computer name and object names for each object.

Logs are used to collect data over time. The logs can be activated with the Data From option and reviewed. Performance Monitor treats a log file exactly the same as current data, allowing you to selectively chart and report from a log file. Log files are really handy for collecting information from several systems on a network over time.

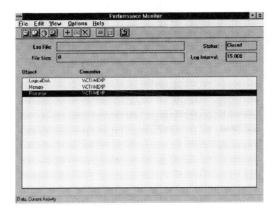

Log Window

The Log Options dialog is shown below. This dialog allows you to start or stop collections to the log file and specify the log file name.

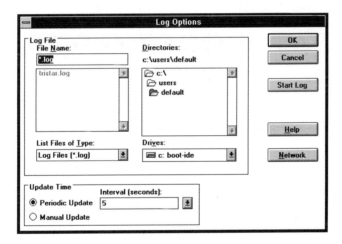

Log Options Dialog

The Update Time box works the same way as the Update Time fields in the other Performance Monitor options. The two buttons determine whether the log is automatically updated (the time value specifies how often the update is performed) or whether you must manually tell Performance Monitor when to update the log.

Report Window

The Report window displays information dynamically. Report is a handy tool for tracking counters as they change in real-time.

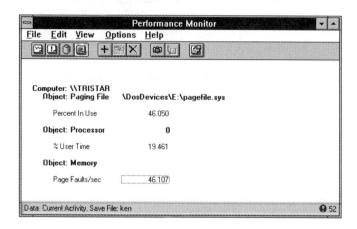

Report Window

The Report Options dialog allows you to select the time interval for automatic updates to the report display. There is no manual update option for Report.

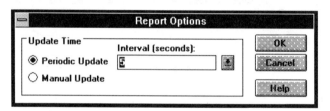

Report Options Dialog

Maintaining Data Entries

Adding a Data Entry

The data items in Performance Monitor windows are user-selectable. The Add button on the toolbar will display the appropriate Add dialog for the current window. The dialog for the Chart window is explained below. The Add dialogs for the Log, Report, and Alert windows are similar to the Add Chart dialog.

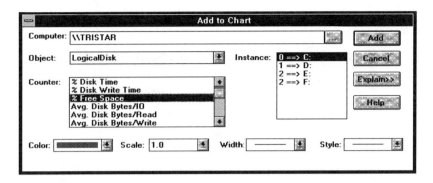

Add to Chart Dialog

The Add dialog is used to select the entries to monitor. A wide variety of entries can be displayed, and you can choose entries from different computers to display at the same time. For instance, you might want to monitor processor activity for all systems in a network or certain workgroup. Another situation might require monitoring physical disk usage across computers or on one system.

The Explain button will provide a brief explanation of the selected entry and counters. The next figure illustrates the Add to Chart dialog after clicking the same Explain button.

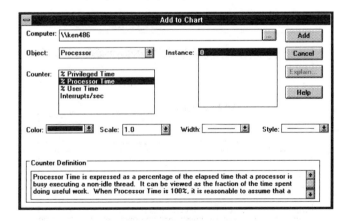

Add to Chart Dialog with Counter Definition

Performance Monitor tracks counters and other statistics for every resource or process on the system. This means that if you have four disk drives, you should be able to see statistics for each drive. The following figure shows the Add to Chart dialog with the

LogicalDisk entry selected. Notice that it shows four "Instances" of this object: C:, D:, E:, and F:. This is because there are four logical disks attached to the workstation.

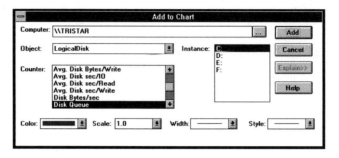

Add to Chart Dialog with Logical Disk Counters

By tracking each instance of an object, Performance Monitor allows you to carefully monitor your system. For instance, you could track the performance of different disks with the same workload in the Chart window. You can also track programs that are running on your system by looking at the Process object.

Editing a Displayed Entry

The Edit dialog allows you to edit a displayed entry and its parameters and is the same as the Add dialog. The dialog displayed is for the currently selected window and the selected item in that window. The following figure shows each Edit Alert Entry dialog.

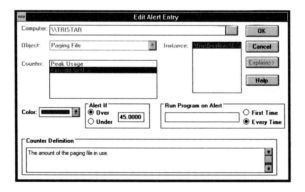

Edit Alert Entry Dialog

You can change the displayed characteristics of a data item on this dialog. Once you have changed a parameter, click OK, and the change will take place immediately.

Removing a Data Entry

The Delete button on the toolbar is used to delete an item from a window. Once a data item is removed, it is no longer updated or displayed. To delete an item:

1. Select the item in the window.

2. Click the Delete button on the toolbar.

Updating Displayed Data Entries

The Options dialog defines how often the data items in each window are updated. The interval can range from 1 to 3,600 seconds (1 hour).

At times you may want to be sure that you are looking at current data instead of stale data. You can be certain that all data is updated by clicking the Update button on the toolbar.

USING PERFORMANCE MONITOR

The figure below shows a Performance Monitor Chart window that is tracking page faults (small spikes), user mode processor time, and several other items. This graphic illustrates the power and ease of use of Performance Monitor. Notice how the graphic displays a line graph in the top of the window, and the lower section of the window contains a nice legend, complete with several details on the entry. This type of display provides a tremendous amount of information at a glance, allowing a system manager or user to quickly get a handle on system problems.

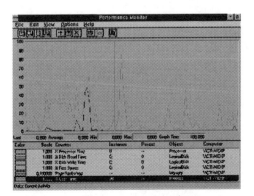

Chart Window - Sample Data

The following example monitors the amount of time the system spends in User mode (actually performing work for the user), the cache success rate, and the number of sessions on the system.

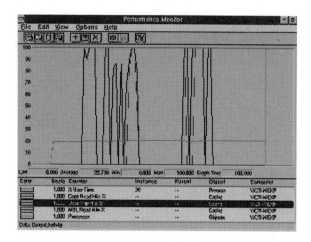

Performance Monitor Chart Window

Type of Data Monitored

Performance Monitor can monitor a tremendous amount of information about your NT system. This includes standard NT counters and application counters logged by the application programs.

Although Performance Monitor is powerful, it can also be confusing to a new user or someone that is not intimate with NT's internal counters and process. For example, the following list contains the events that can be monitored concerning just the operation of the NT cache subsystem:

Async Copy Reads/sec	Fast Read Resource Misses/sec
Async Copy Maps/sec	Fast Reads/sec
Async Fast Reads/sec	Lazy Write Flushes/sec
Async MDL Reads/sec	Lazy Write Pages/sec
Copy Read Hits %	MDL Read Hits %
Copy Reads/sec	Pin Read Hits %
Data Flush pages/sec	Pin Reads/sec
Data Flushes/sec	Sync Data Maps/sec
Data Map Hits %	Sync Data Maps/sec
Data Map Pins/sec	Sync MDL Reads/sec
Fast Read Not Possible/sec	Sync Pin Reads/sec

Any of these events can be added to a chart with a few clicks of the mouse. The cache statistics represented here are only one of the subsystems that can be monitored. Other subsystems include the systems processors, the disk systems, memory, network functions, server functions, and processes running on the system. This is not an all-inclusive list.

Performance Monitor tracks multiple "instances" of each object where applicable. An instance is an actual occurrence of a particular counter for an object. See the Adding a Data Entry section earlier in this chapter for more information about this subject.

Let's look at a few of the objects and counters available from Performance Monitor and see how they can be used. This discussion is not intended to be an in-depth review of Performance Monitor objects, but it should serve as an indicator of the types of information available in Performance Monitor and how the information can be used.

Processor Time

The Processor object is a useful object to track for heavily loaded systems. The % Processor Time counter tracks the time the processor spends performing useful work, in other words, actually running a process that is performing a task (either a system or application program). When the processor time is approaching 100 percent, a faster processor or a multiple-processor machine will probably improve the performance of your system.

The Explain button on the Add and Edit dialogs provides a description that is nearly identical to the explanation above. You should use the Explain button when you notice an obscure counter that is showing high values.

The % User Time counter indicates how much time the processor spends running user-mode programs.

Process Information

The Process object tracks counters for each process running on the system. There are a variety of counters available for this object that we have seen for other objects, such as page fault counters, pool usage counters, and processor usage.

The Base Priority counter is useful for finding out the priority level of the processes running on your system. The following figure shows the Chart window displaying the Base Priority for several active processes.

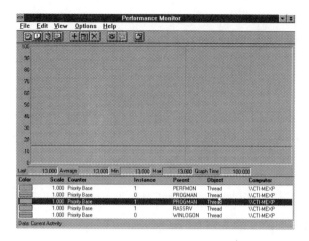

Chart Window with Base Priority

Performance Monitor also tracks resource usage counters by process. If you want to find out which process is hogging the system or what is happening when a process executes, %Processor Time, %Privileged Time, and %User Time can be useful.

Disk Performance

The counters for disk performance must be turned on with the DISKPERF command in order for Performance Monitor to track disk statistics. You must be a member of the Administrators group to execute this command. The format of this command is:

```
C:\> DISKPERF -Y
```

You can also use this command to turn on or off disk statistics tracking on another system by adding the computer name to the command:

```
C:\> DISKPERF -Y  \\PURCH1
```

The -N option turns tracking off:

```
C:\> DISKPERF -N
```

The changes made with DISKPERF do not take effect until the next time the system is rebooted.

Physical Disk

The Physical Disk object tracks information at the physical disk level. In other words, it monitors the disks attached to your system and records data by disk, not by partition. For instance, on a system with three physical disk drives and four logical drives (C:, D:, E:, F:), the Physical Disk object will track data for drives 0, 1, and 2.

For this information to be useful, you must know which disks are which on your system and what logical drives are located on each disk. Guess what? NT can help with this as well. The next figure shows the Add to Chart dialog with the LogicalDisk object selected. The Instances box will list the physical disk number followed by the logical drive letter. This figure shows us that disk 0 is C:, disk 1 is D:, and disk 2 is E: and F:.

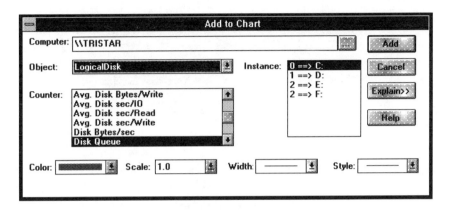

Add to Chart with LogicalDisk Showing Physical Disk

Armed with this information, you can begin to test your disk drives for things like the amount of time each disk takes to read data (Average Disk Bytes/Read) or the length of time one disk is busy compared to another (Disk Queue). The Disk Queue counter can be used to find out which disks are receiving the highest loading. Corrective action may be to restructure the files located on the disk drives to spread the load across multiple disk drives.

Logical Disk

The Logical Disk object tracks things that occur on the logical drives on your system. This type of information includes some of the counters that are available in the Physical Disk object, including Disk Write Time, Disk Read Time, and Disk Queue, and things such as % Free Space, Free Megabytes, and a number of counters that report disk performance information.

The following figure shows the Alert view with some interesting information.

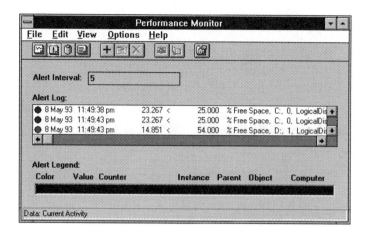

Alert View with Logical Disk Counters

The figure shows several alerts concerning the amount of free space on a logical disk drive (%Free Space): C: < 25% free, D: < 54% free. Notice that the logical drive letter is displayed, followed by the physical disk number. Setting this option is a neat way to be alerted when the available space on a disk is getting marginal. The Free Megabyte counter is also useful for tracking when a disk is below a certain minimum amount of free space. Or, maybe you want to check several shares on your network and find out which one has the most free space. Add a counter to the Chart window for a Logical Disk Counter for each system and their disks, and you will have a real-time graphical indicator. Save the configuration to a file, and you can repeat the test with a few clicks of the mouse to reload the settings file.

Using Log Files

Setting Up and Maintaining a Log File

Using a log to track information allows you to collect data over time and review that data on a regular basis. Tracking data over time is the only way to accurately monitor the performance of a system, because it provides a historic view of the data during actual use of the system.

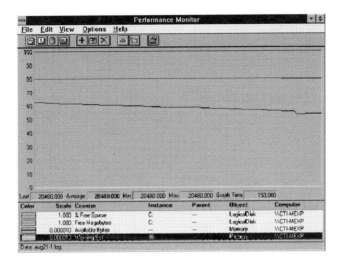

Performance Monitor Chart Displaying a Log File

The illustration above shows the chart window displaying data from a log file. This log file collected data for approximately 10 minutes. Data can be collected for any length of time, limited only by disk space for the log file. Performance Monitor collects data in a log by updating the file periodically. The default update interval is every 5 seconds.

Starting a log file is very simple:

1. Select the Log window.

2. Select your Log file.

   ◆ Start a new log by selecting File/New Log.

   ◆ Open an existing log by selecting File/Open.

3. Add your selections to the log.

   ◆ Click the Add button.

   ◆ Make your selections from the Add dialog.

   ◆ Click Done when you are finished adding selections.

4. Save the Log - File/Save.

5. Start the Log - Options/Log.

   ◆ Click the Start Log button.

Maintaining the Log File

You can review the log file and change log file objects any time by switching to the Log window and opening the log file.

Viewing Data from a Log File

Once the log file is created, you can switch from viewing current data to viewing data from a log file. Remember that you can set up more than one log file and that you can have different configurations for log files. All Performance Monitor windows perform the same when you view data from a log file, as they do when viewing current data.

The Data From dialog is used to switch between viewing current data and a log file. This dialog is available on all Performance Monitor windows via the Options/Data From menu selection.

Data From Dialog

Select the Current Activity button to view current system activity or click Log File to view a log file. The **...** button beside the log file name (perfmon.log, in this example) will display the open dialog, allowing you to choose another log file.

Once you have selected the log file, you can switch to another view. You may want to change the data items in the display, depending on what items are displayed in the window and what objects were logged in the log file.

Bookmarks

Bookmarks can be set in a log file to mark important points in the file. A bookmark is designed to be a quick reference note, just like the traditional paper bookmark. The easiest way to set a bookmark is by clicking on bookmark in the toolbar, which will display the Bookmark dialog. Enter your comments and click OK. Bookmarks are available only after a log file has been started.

You can use bookmarks as starting and ending points for viewing data from a log file using the Input Log File Timeframe dialog.

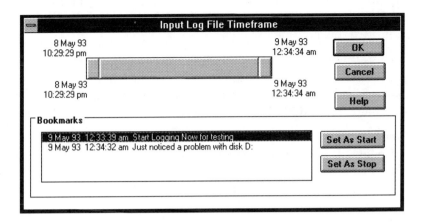

Input Log File Timeframe

The bookmarks are used by clicking on a bookmark and then clicking Set As Start or Set As Stop.

Beginning and Ending Times

Once you have selected a log file, you can fine-tune the start and stop times that are displayed. Changing the start and stop times allows you to select a range of data to view. The Edit/Times Window displays the Input Log File Timeframe dialog, which allows you to set the beginning and ending points from the log. Selecting times in this window only changes the information displayed; it does not affect the data in the log file.

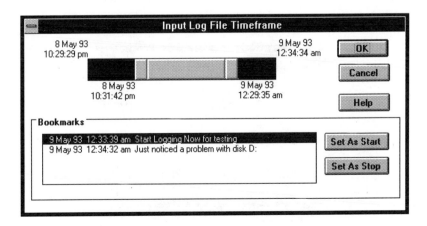

Input Log File Timeframe (Time Window)

To change the start time, drag the left end of the time bar to the right or left. You will see the start time change as you drag the bar. The more data you have in the log, the more sensitive the movements will be.

The end time is changed by dragging the right end of the bar. After you have set the time range, you can click anywhere in the middle of the bar and drag the time range forward or backward. This is very useful for looking at a set period of time and moving it forward or backward quickly.

Another nice feature of this window is the ability to use bookmarks for beginning and ending points. If you carefully record bookmarks when you notice problems or changes in your system, you can quickly select these bookmarks for your start and end times and begin your research from a known point.

Using Alerts

Alerts are a handy tool for trapping errors over time as they occur. Alerts are triggered when an item exceeds the value entered in the Edit Alert dialog.

Use care when you decide which items to monitor for alerts and what value should trigger the alert. Usually the first tendency is to trap a number of alerts and to set the triggers at a fairly low level. This leads to a tremendous number of alert log entries that will usually be very difficult to monitor or decipher. Starting with a few alerts and setting the alert values at a tight level will generate an alert log with a limited number of entries that will be easy to monitor. Once you have a handle on the problems that triggered these alerts, you can begin to slowly add new alerts or open up the alert trigger values.

The Alert window can be used to trap any of the items supported by Performance Monitor.

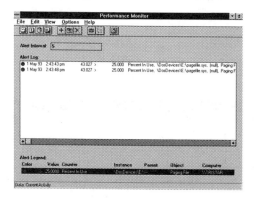

Alert Window

Setting Up Program Manager Icons

Performance Monitor is one of those tools that is especially useful when you spend some time configuring your system for it. Using the program groups in Program Manager, you can set up icons that will load Performance Monitor and workspace files at the same time. This makes it very easy to build a configuration panel by creating a program group with nothing but Performance Monitor icons that point to separate setup files for different purposes. The steps to create this group are:

1. Set up the Program Manager group (only for new groups).

   ◆ File/New in Program Manager.

   ◆ Select Personal or Common Group.

2. File/New in Program Manager.

   ◆ Select Program Item.

3. Click Browse and select the settings file you wish to add (name.PMW, name.PMC, etc.) as the command line for the option.

You may have to associate the file with PERFMON.EXE in File Manager (File/Associate) before performing this task.

The following figure shows the Administrative group with new icons for directly accessing either a chart window with Logical Disk counters or a chart window with Memory counters.

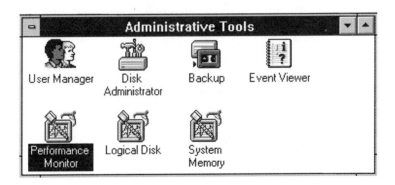

Administrative Group with Icons

CHAPTER 8

Event Viewer

INTRODUCTION TO EVENT VIEWER

NT is one of the first systems that has provided a common system mechanism for logging problem information by both applications and system components. Many systems have provided means for logging security or system events and sometimes both, but none has really provided a cohesive mechanism like NT for managing all types of event logs.

The event logs track information about the events that take place on the NT system. Events are written (logged) in the event log by NT programs and application programs as they operate. The type of event determines to which log the event information is written. User Manager audit settings determine what types of audit events are logged.

Event information is logged into three types of event logs: System, Security, and Application. The following table covers the types of information contained and the systems that record information in each log.

Log Type	Description of Events
System	Events in the System log are recorded by NT system programs as they occur in the system. Examples of this type of event are problems during startup or the failure of an NT system operation because of a resource problem.
Security	The Security log records information about security-related events that occur during NT's operation. The exact events that are recorded depend on the audit settings in User Manager and the resources you have selected for auditing with File Manager and Print Manager.
Application	Applications may also record information in event logs by logging them in the Application log. This log records any event that may have significance for a particular application. For instance, an application could record problems that occur within the application when trying to access files or possibly printer errors.

Event Viewer is the tool used for managing and viewing information about these wonderful logs. The Event Viewer interface provides a simple format for selecting the type of log and the functions to perform on the log. A currently active log is the normal display, although Event Viewer can store archives of a log for display at a later date.

Event Viewer displays information from a log file when you open a file. Once the log file is opened, the information is not updated unless you specifically request that the information be refreshed from the View Menu or by pressing F5. The lack of updating is a major difference between Event Viewer and Performance Monitor, because the latter displays information as it happens, unless you are reviewing a log file.

Options are also available for managing the size of your log files and what happens to records in the log when a log file reaches its maximum size. You can also clear a log file in Event Viewer.

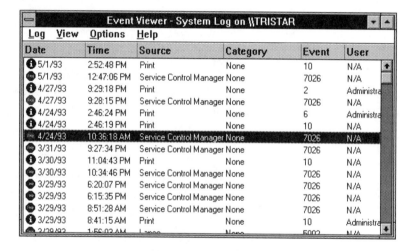

Event Viewer

Notice how event viewer flags each event with an icon that indicates that classification of the event. This gives you a quick indication of the status of the events in the log. The icons are:

Icon   **Description**

Error — This icon represents a critical error in your system, such as the failure of a device driver at startup.

Warning — The warning icon indicates events that are important (such as things that may cause future problems) but do not necessarily stop your system.

Information — The Information icon represents informative events that are usually the result of a successful operation.

Success Audit — This icon indicates successful audited events.

Failure Audit — The Failure Audit icon represents unsuccessful audited events.

Displaying Event Details

The Details dialog will display information from NT and the program that logged the event. The Details dialog will usually contain a text description of the event and may optionally display other data that may be used by technical support specialists that support the software that logged the event. Double-click, or select the event and press enter to display the dialog. You can access the details of an event by double-clicking the event.

The next figure shows an Event Detail dialog displaying information about an event failure that was logged when NT booted.

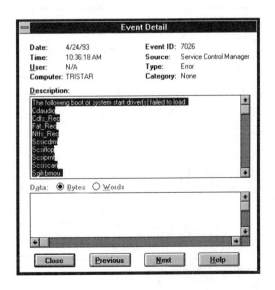

Event Details - Startup Error

The next figure shows an Event Detail dialog that contains information about a printer audit event.

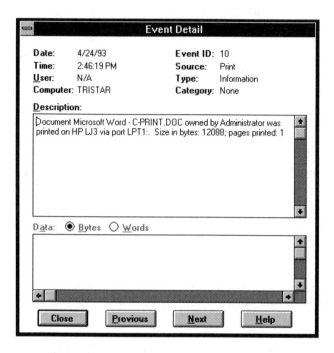

Event Detail Dialog - Example of Printer Auditing

Notice the level of detail in this log entry, even down to the application that created the document and the document file name. As applications are developed that take advantage of the logging services of NT, we should see more and more detail entered in the event log.

The Next and Previous buttons are very handy, especially when you have filtered the log to show only a certain type of event. These buttons provide quick access to the next or last event in the log when you click the appropriate button. When events are filtered to one particular type or classification, scrolling through the events with Next and Previous allows you to quickly review the details and pick out potential problems. For more information, see the Filtering Events section of this chapter.

Starting to Use Event Viewer

The first step is to turn off Options/Save Settings on Exit. Leaving this option on will cause Event Viewer to save your settings each time you exit. I prefer to leave this setting off and manually save settings from the Log menu. This prevents me from starting Event Viewer and having a different set of settings each time.

Refreshing the Display

Event Viewer displays information that was current at the time the log was opened. The View/Refresh option refreshes the display from the event log, including all events that occurred since the log was opened. F5 is the shortcut to this command.

Managing Log Files

Event Viewer shows only one event log at a time. The Log menu provides access to commands to select which log to display and perform other log functions. These functions include selecting which type of log to view, opening a log file, selecting an event log on another NT system, clearing events from a log, archiving a log file (save as) and defining settings for Event Manager. The Log menu is shown below.

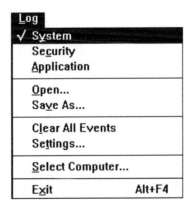

Log Menu

Selecting a Log

Selecting System, Security, or Application determines the event log for viewing. The log will be displayed, and all Event Viewer actions will operate on that log. You must be a member of the Administrators group to view a Security log.

You can select a log from another computer by first selecting the remote system by choosing Log/Select Computer and then choosing the log type.

The File/Open option allows you to select an archived event log for viewing. Archived logs behave like the standard log files except that the Refresh option is not available.

Archiving an Event Log

The Log/Save As selection is used to archive an event log. Log files can be saved in Log File format, Text File format, or Comma-Delimited format. Archived files in Log File format can be used only by Event Viewer, while the Text File or Comma-Delimited format can be read by many other applications such as Word for Windows or Excel.

The record format for both Text File and Comma-Delimited format is Date, Time, Source, Type, Category, Event, User, Computer, Description.

Saving information in Comma-Delimited format is useful for using in a spreadsheet or database program. See Chapter 6 for more information.

Archiving event logs in Log File format is useful for saving old event logs for later review. This can be useful when you have a particular problem such as a printer or device problem or possibly a security problem. Having the event log around may be useful if a similar problem occurs later, because you can refer to the old log, including bookmarks, for clues to researching the current problem.

Clearing an Event Log

The Log/Clear All Events option will clear the events from an event log. After selecting this option, a dialog allows you to save an archive of the current log file.

Event Log Settings

The Log/Settings option displays a dialog for setting options for your event logs. These settings affect the size of your event logs and the methods used by NT when the event log becomes full. The dialog for the Settings menu option is shown below.

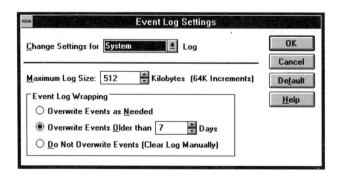

Log Options Dialog

The following table defines what effect the various options have on your event logs.

Option	Description
Change Settings For	The Change Settings For option determines which log settings will be updated.
Maximum Log Size	This option specifies the maximum size of the log file. The default is 512.
Overwrite Events as Needed	This option allows NT to overwrite events as required when the log becomes full. NT does this by overwriting the oldest event each time. This is the default option.
Overwrite Events Older Than	This option allows you to enter a number of days to retain events before they are overwritten. Reducing the retention period is one of the methods for reinstating logging for a full log. The other option is clearing the log. The default is 7 days.
Do Not Overwrite Events (Clear Log Manually)	This option will cause NT never to overwrite an event. Use this option only if you cannot afford to miss an event record. This option also means you must clear the event log manually. The NT documentation suggests that you also select Halt System When Full in user Manager Auditing Policies if you select the Do Not Overwrite Events option.

Displaying and Finding Events

The View menu provides options for controlling how you view the events in the currently open log. The All Events option on this menu allows you to select a subset of the log or all of the events in the log. The Newest First and Oldest First options select the order in which the events are displayed.

View Menu

The two check marks indicate that all events are displayed and that newer items appear first in the log. The View menu is a handy place to check the status of the sort order and filtering status each time you start Event Viewer. This is especially important if you have Save Settings on Exit checked in the Options menu.

Display All Events and Sorting the Log

The View/All Events option is the default filtering selection and causes Event Viewer to display All Events in the event log. You may need to select this option to return the display to the All Events setting after you have done extensive sorting or filtering or when you notice that the title bar displays Filtered. If you have saved your settings from a previous setting, All Events may not be the default display.

The View/Newest First and Oldest First options specify the sort order for the currently viewed event log. Selecting one of these options does not affect how the events are stored in the log file, although they will affect how the events are sorted when a log file is archived. The default display is Newest First, because this is the order in which the events are recorded.

Filtering Events

The View/Filter option determines which events are displayed by Event Viewer. The default display when Event Viewer loads is for all events unless you have selected a filtering option during a previous session of Event Viewer and your changes were saved from that session. Event Viewer will show Filtered in the title bar when filtering is on, and the Filter option on the menu will have a check mark beside it.

The Filter option is a key feature of Event Viewer when you are trying to track down system errors. Filtering allows you to restrict the display to only events and time periods that are of interest.

For instance, let's say you have been out of town and return on 7/6/1993 to find a problem has occurred with a printer attached to your system. After a little investigation, you find out that the problem started on 7/1/1993. Let's also assume that you had Failure Auditing turned on for printer events.

If you did not have Failure Auditing turned on for the problem printer, you will not find any audits in the log. Audit failures are logged only when Failure Audits have been turned on and a file or printer has users or groups selected for auditing.

First, pull up the Filter dialog (View/Filter) and select 07/1/1993 for the View From date. Next, Turn off all Types except for Failure Audits. Select Print for our source and click OK. You should now see a manageable list of Print events that occurred within the time period (6 days) and were logged as Print Failures.

Look through the events in the list and see if there are any common problems. Once you find a suspicious or interesting event, double-click the event to displays the Details dialog. From this dialog you can use the Previous and Next buttons to move through the details one at a time. The Filtering dialog is shown below.

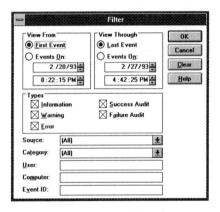

Filter Dialog

The following table describes the options on the Filter dialog.

Option	Description
View From	This option selects events for viewing based on the View From data and time. All events after this date are displayed.
View Through	This option displays events up to a certain date and time.
Type	The Type box lists check boxes for selecting event types to filter.
Source	This option displays all events for a particular source such as a system program or application program.
Category	This option displays events for a particular category. Categories are defined by the source logging the event. The NT documentation lists examples such as logon and logoff.
User	This option displays events for a specific user.
Computer	This option displays events for a particular computer.
Event ID	The Event ID displays all events that match the Event ID.

Searching for a Specific Event

View/Find (F3) allows you to search the for certain events. You can search by the options that were used in the Filter dialog plus several other options. The dialog also allows you to search for descriptions by entering partial descriptions in the Description field.

This dialog is very handy when you want to look for an event in the log. It is also easy to remember the shortcut to this command, because F4 seems to be the favorite find key within most Windows applications.

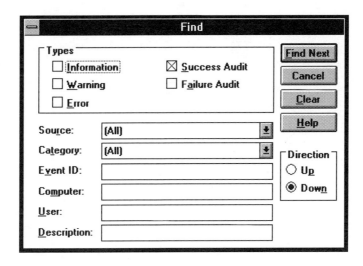

Find Dialog

The following table describes the options on the Find dialog.

Option	Description
Type	The Type box lists check boxes for selecting event types to filter.
Up	Up will cause Find to look for events from the current event backward.
Down	Down will cause Find to look for events from the current event forward.
Source	This option displays all events for a particular source such as a system program or application program.
Category	This option displays events for a particular category. Categories are defined by the source logging the event. The NT documentation lists examples such as logon and logoff.
Event ID	The Event ID displays all events that match the Event ID.
Computer	This option displays events for a particular computer.
User	This field selects events by user account name.
Description	The Description field can be used to find an event by entering the entire description or part of the text contained in the description.

CHAPTER 9

User Manager

INRODUCTION TO USER MANAGER

The NT User Manager serves as a management utility for controlling user accounts, groups, and audit settings. User Manager's features are similar to the features of many network operating systems' user management software, such as NetWare's Syscon. User Manager is easy to use and adds a few new wrinkles to user management by adding support for user policies.

User Manager is typical of many NT programs that bring together the features of various operating systems and roll them together. The graphical interface brings to mind some of the Macintosh administrative tools, while the support for user account groups is common to many systems. Features such as user policies round out the environment and provide tools for effectively managing an NT system. The main User Manager screen is shown below.

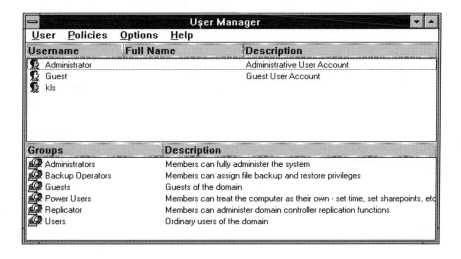

User Manager

You will notice from the graphical nature of the screen how User Manager was designed for ease of use. Most operations are accomplished by dragging and dropping an icon or selecting several items and clicking a button. User Manager and the other NT utilities bring a new face to workstation and network management.

The layout of the screen is very clean, with user accounts listed in the top half of the window and groups shown in the lower section. NT has standard icons for users and groups which prove useful in several applications — such as User Manager, File Manager, and Print Manager — when you are selecting users and/or groups from a list. The icons quickly identify whether the list item is a user account or a group. These two icons are shown below.

     This icon identifies a user account.

     This icon identifies a group.

Chapter 6 has an in-depth discussion on user accounts, groups, and other items that relate to User Manager functions. Before creating new accounts, make sure you read and understand the related topics in that chapter.

User Manager and NT Security

User Manager uses the NT security system to determine who can perform a given task. As with other NT programs, administrators can perform any User Manager task. Power users can create user accounts and groups. They can also modify and delete groups they have created. Users (accounts that are members of the Users group) can create groups and modify and delete groups they have created. An account must be a member of the Administrators or Power Users group to create or manage accounts.

The implementation of the security system is not totally consistent because of the way users are prohibited from performing actions. Many times an option will be shown as unavailable to users who do not have access to the option. At other times, the user can perform the command, but NT ignores the command and does not execute it.

Managing User Accounts

Adding a User Account

Users can be added one at a time, or you may wish to create template accounts that allow you to create duplicate user accounts very quickly. The method you select should depend on the type of system or network that you have and how your system will be used.

The New User dialog allows you to add a user account by entering the username, full name, description, and password. You can also disable the account and select whether the user may change his or her password. Two command buttons are available for selecting groups for the account and accessing the account's profile.

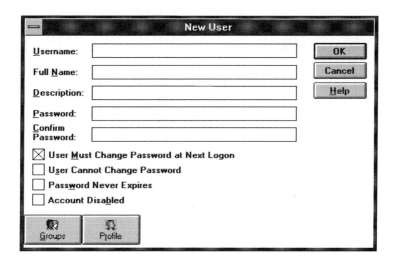

New User Dialog

The options in the New User dialog are described in the following table.

Option	Description
Username	The Username field specifies the logon name for the account.
Full Name	The Full Name field is used to define the full name for the user of the account. This field is informational only.
Description	This field describes the account. This field is informational only.
Password	The Password field defines the password for the account. See the discussion on passwords in Chapter 6.
Confirmation	The Confirmation field is used to verify the password for the account. When you enter a password for an account, you must enter the password again in the Confirmation field.
User Must Change Password at Next Logon	Checking this box forces the user to change his or her password the next time the user logs on.
User Cannot Change Password	Checking this box prevents the user form ever changing the password.

Password Never Expires	Checking this box causes the password never to expire. This setting overrides User Must Change Password at Next Logon. It also overrides the Maximum Password Age setting in the Account Policy.
Account Disabled	Checking this box disables a user account.
Groups Button	The Groups button displays the group selection list, allowing you to select groups for the user.
Profile Button	The Profile button displays the Profile dialog, allowing you to enter the home directory and logon script for a user.

Creating a single-user account is straightforward:

1. Select User/New User.

2. Enter the following fields:

   ◆ Username.

   ◆ Full Name (optional).

   ◆ Account Description (optional).

   ◆ Password (in both the Password and Confirmation boxes).

3. Select the desired account options:

   ◆ User Must Change Password at Next Logon.

   ◆ User Cannot Change Password.

   ◆ Account Disabled.

4. Select the groups for the account by clicking the Groups button.

5. Enter the home directory and logon script by clicking the Profile button.

Creating users one at a time is useful for a system that is used at home or in the office and has only a few accounts. These types of systems will probably have three or four accounts and a very limited number of groups. Security will typically not be a big deal for most of these systems.

User Profile

Once you have filled in the basic user properties, you are ready to fill in the Profile properties. These properties are the Logon script name and the home directory specification. The User Environment Profile dialog is shown below.

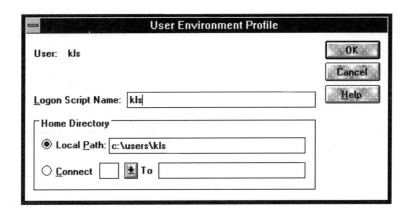

User Environment Profile Dialog

After you enter the Logon Script Name and Home Directory specification, click OK. User Manager will automatically create the home directory or display an error message if it can't. The logon script name only references the logon script; User Manager does not verify that the script exists or perform any other actions with the name.

See the discussions on home directories and logon scripts in Chapter 6.

Adding Accounts to Groups

The Groups button on the New User dialog is used to add an account to a group. Click Add, and the Group Membership dialog will be displayed.

Buttons on the Group Membership dialog provide a quick means for performing several tasks. The Add button is used to add the user account to groups of which the account is not a member. To add the user to a group, select the group in the Not Member Of box and click Add.

You can remove the user account from a group by selecting the group in the Member Of box and clicking Remove.

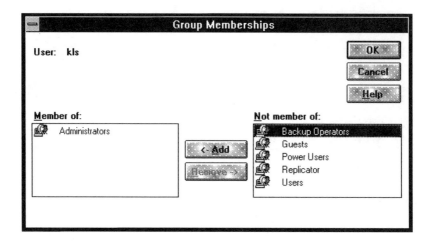

Group Membership Dialog

You can also add or remove a user from a group using the drag-and-drop method from in this dialog. You must click on the icon and not the name to drag and drop a group or user. The following steps show how to perform this task:

1. To add an account to a group:

   ◆ Select the group icon in the Not Member Of box.

   ◆ Drag the icon and drop it in the Member Of box.

2. To remove an account from a group:

   ◆ Select the group icon in the Member Of box.

   ◆ Drag the icon and drop it in the Not Member Of box.

Copying a User Account

It is usually easier to create a user account by copying an existing account that has the same general format. For instance, if you need to create an account that is a member of ten groups and uses a common login script, it will be much easier to copy an existing account that uses the same groups and login script.

The steps to create a copy of an account are:

1. Select an account from the main window.

2. Select User/Copy (F8).

3. Configure the account in the Copy Of dialog, then click OK.

The Copy Of dialog is shown below.

Copy Of Dialog

If you have a large number of users and/or a sizable network, you will probably want to create template accounts. Using template accounts allows you to build one account for each type of user, including user groups. Once the template account is created, you can create an identical account very quickly and be assured that you have not missed a critical step or left the user out of an important group.

When you copy a user account, User Manager creates the home directory based on the following rule: If the last component of the home directory path is the same as the username, the user's home directory will be created with the same name as the username. If the last component is different from the username, the home directory will be created with the name of this component.

NT provides a variable named %USERNAME% to make creating multiple user accounts easier. The %USERNAME% variable is used by specifying %USERNAME% as the last component in the home directory field. User Manager will create the home directory for each user by substituting the account's username for the directory name. This variable is useful when you are changing a number of accounts at one time. It is also useful in template accounts for automatically creating the user's home directory from his or her account name. There is one caution when using %USERNAME%: If the parent home directory is on a FAT volume, you may run into problems. NT allows usernames that are longer than eight characters and contain characters that are not allowed in FAT systems.

When User Manager tries to create an account profile with an invalid login directory name, it will warn you that you must create the home directory manually.

A template account is created by the following steps:

1. Select User/New.

2. Name the account using a descriptive name that includes the letters TMP at the beginning of the name. This will cause all the template accounts to be grouped together whenever the accounts are listed.

3. Fill in the description for the account.

4. Enter the user profile information.

Use the %USERNAME% parameter for the last part of the home directory. If one of the parent directories does not exist, it must be created before adding users with the template.

5. Add the account to the desired groups.

6. Click OK.

Now that the template account has been created, let's see how it can be used:

1. Select the template account to use.

2. Select User/Copy (F8).

3. Fill in the Username, Full Name, Password, and Confirm Password fields.

4. Click OK.

Changing User Account Properties

A user account's properties can be accessed by simply double-clicking a user account or by selecting User/Properties, which displays the User Properties dialog.

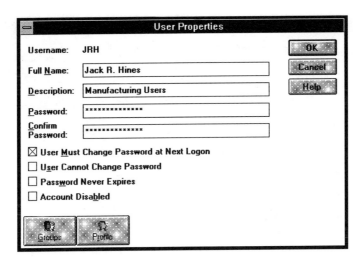

User Properties Dialog

This is basically the same dialog that is used for a new user. You can tell that this dialog is for an existing user because the Username is not available for editing. The Username for an account cannot be changed after the account is created without using the Rename function. The fields and options on this dialog are the same as those for a new user.

Modifying More Than One Account at a Time

You can also modify more than one account at the same time, allowing you to change selected properties for all users at once. This process becomes tricky with more accounts and when users have different options selected. Be careful: This option is very powerful and very dangerous.

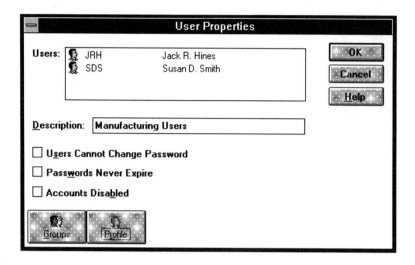

User Properties with Multiple Accounts Selected

If the selected accounts have the same description, the description will appear in the Description field, as in this example. If one or more accounts have a different description, the description will be blank.

If the selected accounts have the same option, the option will be displayed. If one or more accounts have a different option, that option will be grayed out.

Remember, whichever option you change (including the description) will be the same for every selected account.

Now for the good news: Selecting multiple accounts is a nice way to change options for many users at the same time. Let's say you need to flag several accounts so that their passwords never expire. The steps are very simple:

1. Select the accounts.

2. Select User/Properties.

3. Change the desired options.

4. Click OK.

Managing Groups for Multiple Accounts

When you select more than one account and click the Groups button on the Properties dialog, User Manager displays a variation of the Group Memberships dialog. The options in this dialog are explained in the following table:

Option	Description
Users	This box shows the selected users.
All Are Members Of	This box lists groups that all selected users are members of.
Not All Are Members Of	This box lists groups that not all selected users are members of.

To change group memberships for multiple user accounts, follow these steps:

1. Select the accounts.

2. Select the Groups button.

3. Change the groups for the accounts. Drag the groups from one box to the other or click Add/Remove. See the discussion below on removing groups.

4. Click OK.

When you want to remove the selected users from a group of which some are members and some are not, you must perform an extra step. Complete the steps above, add the group to the All Are Members Of box, and click OK. Then select the Groups button again and drag the group to the Not All Are Members Of box.

Renaming a User Account

The User/Rename function is used to rename a user account. The dialog is shown below.

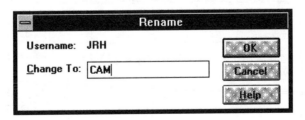

Rename Dialog

This dialog changes the logon name of the account but does not change the account ID. If a user leaves your department or company, you can rename the account for the person that replaces the user, and the new user will still have access to all the resources the original user did.

Removing Access to a User Account

User Manager provides two options for removing access to an account: disabling and deleting the account.

The steps to disable an account are:

1. Select the accounts.

2. Display the User Properties dialog by selecting User/Properties.

3. Click the Account Disabled box.

To delete an account:

1. Select the account.

2. Press the DEL key or select User/Delete.

Accounts should almost always be disabled instead of deleted. Disabling an account prohibits access to the account but allows you to reactivate and then rename the account at a later time.

Managing Groups

Adding a Group

Adding local groups to an NT workstation is very simple: Select User/New Local Group, and the following dialog will be displayed.

New Local Group Dialog

You can complete the process quickly by entering the Group Name and the Description fields and clicking OK. This whole process takes only 5 or 10 seconds. However, read the section on groups in Chapter 6 and think through the organization of the groups on your system.

Notice the user Guest shows up in the Members box, and we haven't even defined the group. This is because User Manager will automatically place the selected users in the group. You can select either a single user, as shown, or multiple users. You can also add users from this dialog by selecting the Add button, which will display the Add Users and Groups dialog.

The Show Names button will display the full name for the user accounts.

Changing a Group's Properties
Properties of a group can be changed by double-clicking a group or selecting a group and selecting User/Properties. The only property you can change is the description and the users in the group. The group name cannot be changed.

Deleting a Group
The Delete command from the User menu is used to delete a local group. Deleting a group does not delete the members of the group but removes all permissions and rights of the group and deletes the group.

The NT documentation issues the same cautions about deleting a group as it does for deleting a user account, because groups are also known by a security ID. If you delete a group and then recreate one with the same name, the new group will be different and will not have access to the same file. There is no way to disable a group unless you remove all the user accounts in the group or remove all permissions for the group.

Policies

The Policies menu provides access to the Account, User Rights, and Audit policies. Policy options are systemwide and provide control over a number of NT events.

Account Policy
The Account policy controls password use by setting parameters that affect passwords and user accounts. The parameters are maximum and minimum password age, minimum password length, and the amount of history that NT tracks for each password.

These parameters control the way passwords are used throughout the entire system.

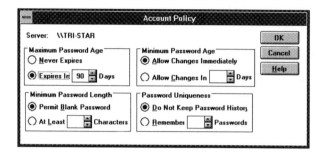

Account Policy Dialog

The descriptions and value ranges for each parameter are:

Option	Description
Maximum Password Age	The maximum time between password changes (1 to 999 days, or never).
Minimum Password Age	The minimum time between password changes (1 to 999 days).
Allow Changes Immediately	This field allows the user to change his or her password changes.
Minimum Password Length	This field specifies the minimum length of the password field (one to fourteen characters).
Permit Blank Passwords	This field permits the account to have no password.
Password Uniqueness (History)	This field specifies how many old passwords against which NT will check the new password (one to eight passwords). New passwords that match an old password in the list cannot be used.

The extent to which you modify the Account Policy settings will depend on the security policies of your organization and the needs of your environment.

User Rights Policy

The user rights policy provides a mechanism for assigning rights explicitly to a user account or group. The NT documentation is very clear in warning users about modifying the user rights policy. Modification of the user rights policy can have disastrous effects on your system if it is not handled appropriately.

NT uses rights to determine which users can perform certain actions. A right is usually assigned to a user by adding the user to a group that has the desired right. Adding a user who should have maintenance rights to the Administrators or Power Users group gives the user the ability to perform the appropriate maintenance duties.

Rights are granted by the Rights dialog box in User Manager. Only administrators can grant rights. The Rights dialog box is also used to remove rights from a user. When you remove a right, make sure you remove the user from any groups that also have the right.

Rights apply to the entire system and are constantly monitored by NT. For instance, a user that does not have Administrators rights will not be able to perform many of the functions in User Manager. Options that are not authorized will not appear, will appear grayed out, or will fail to complete the operation when selected.

A right will always override a permission that applies to a specific object. For instance, a user that is denied access to a file by the No Access permission will still be able to take ownership of the file if the user belongs to the Administrators group.

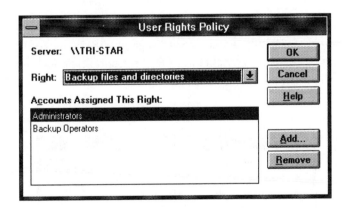

User Rights Dialog

Clicking the Add button will display the following dialog, which allows you to add users or groups to the right. The default display shows only groups in the list. Click the Show Users button, and the user's accounts will be added to the list of groups. In most cases, you should grant rights only to groups. The Members button will be enabled when you select a group account. Clicking on Members will display the members of a group. From the Local Group Membership dialog you can select an account and click Add to add that account to the Add Names box on the previous dialog.

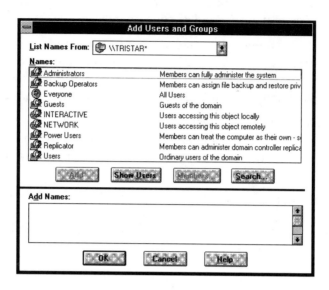

Add Users and Groups Dialog

Audit Policy

The audit policy will probably be used more that the other policy options. The audit policy dialog is used to specify which activities are audited (tracked) by NT. Specify which events are to be audited by clicking the corresponding check box in the Audit Policy dialog. The audit policy takes effect as soon as you have selected the appropriate options.

Audit Policy Dialog

The Audit These Events button must be turned on before you can select any of the options in the Audit These Events box.

Several options are affected under the Audit policy: Logon and Logoff; File and Object Access; Use of User Rights; User and Group Management; Security Policy Changes; Restart, Shutdown, and System; and Process Tracking. The File and Object Access options operate slightly differently than the other options. File and Print resources are not automatically audited by selecting the File and Object Access option. File Manger must be used to specify which files and users are to be tracked, while Print Manager is used to specify which printers and users are tracked. The table below outlines the options. Each option has two possible selections: Success or Failure. Both options can be selected at the same time.

Option	Description
Logon and Logoff	This option turns on monitoring of each user who tries to log on to or off of the workstation.
File and Object Access	This option turns on auditing for files, directories, and printers. Selecting either or both options allows you to select objects and users to audit in File Manager and Print Manager.
Use of User Rights	NT monitors all users who attempt to use a right. This does not include rights related to logon and logoff.
User and Group Management	Turning on either of these options audits changes to user accounts and groups.
Security Policy Changes	This option monitors changes to the system's Security Policy.
Restart, Shutdown, and System	This option causes NT to audit every user who attempts to restart or shut down the system. Users and events will also be audited any time they affect the NT security system or the security log.
Process Tracking	This option turns on auditing for numerous aspects of NT and application program process status.

The NT documentation has a very strong warning concerning one of the Audit options. The Halt System When Security Event Log is Full option is very dangerous and can create havoc on your system. Selecting this option will shut down your system when the security log becomes full. This means that all programs and services stop and the system cannot be used until the log file is cleared or the amount of time events are retained is reduced.

This discussion on audit polices would not be complete without looking at how to establish these policies. Care must be used in selecting audit policies because selecting all options or the incorrect option will quickly clutter your log file with too many entries. This will also eat up your disk space in a hurry, depending on system use and the number of events and resources that are being monitored. The following table illustrates suggested selections.

Audit Option	Success	Failure
Logon and Logoff	Systems that are very secure and/or have strict security policies.	Most systems.
File and Object Access	Systems that are very secure and/or have strict security policies. Systems that are experiencing problems with resource or security changes. File and Print changes can be monitored for specific files/printers as needed.	Most systems.
Use of User Rights	Systems that are very secure and/or have strict security policies.	Most systems.
User and Group Management	Medium-size to large systems and any systems that have moderately strict user management controls.	Most systems.
Security Policy Changes	Very secure systems that have strict security policies.	Most systems.
Restart, Shutdown, and System	Systems that are very secure and/or have strict security policies. Systems that experience high rates of suspicious system shutdowns or restarts.	Most systems.
Process Tracking	Systems that are very secure, are used for program development, or suspect that suspicious activity may be occurring on the system.	Some systems.

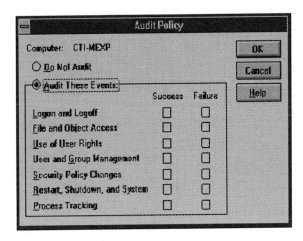

Audit Policy Options

Notice that I suggest turning on Failure Audits on most systems. You should monitor all failures, because they usually point to problems or security risks on your system.

Remember that once you have set your audit policy options, you must monitor the security log in Event Viewer. The more options you select, the more events that will be logged in the security log and the more time you will spend in reviewing the file.

CHAPTER 10

Windows NT Security

INTRODUCTION TO NT SECURITY

NT was designed from the outset as a secure operating system. The NT security model was designed with the following goals:

◆ To provide a minimum impact on Windows API semantics.

◆ To meet the criteria for C2-level security.

◆ To provide an extensible foundation for B-level security without modifications to the existing API.

◆ To provide support for multiuser systems.

◆ To provide support for new object types.

NT provides a number of features for managing the security aspects of your system. Transaction logging, auditing, and file access security are a few of the tools that can be enabled. For instance, File Manager can trigger audits on any file or directory on an NT file system. These audits can be selectively implemented by user or group. File access security is automatically enabled on NTFS volumes, and File Manager can be used to set up permissions on files and directories by user and group. File Manager can also establish security for selected accounts and groups for shared directories.

User Manager can be used to establish security and audit policies for nonfile-related events. Event Viewer can set up alerts to trigger notification or even run a program when a security event occurs. This notification can be on the NT system itself or may be sent over the network. Alerts are also tracked in the Alert log for later review.

The encryption is one-way — a password can't be deciphered — and it occurs when the password is entered in User Manager and when a user logs on. A number of flags can also be set on a password: maximum and minimum password age, minimum length, and history parameters.

NT uses the user ID to validate users against the NT security database. NT automatically defines the initial security of a system when it is installed. At installation time, accounts are created for the initial user, a guest account, and the administrator. The initial user account is placed in the Power Users group. The guest account is normally used when a user tries to connect to a shared resource without supplying a username and password. The guest account should be disabled if you have strict security requirements or you do not want users connecting without a username and password.

Internal Security Structure

NT uses a standard internal scheme to manage all systems resources. Files, processes, semaphores, devices, and so on, are managed as objects through a uniform, consistent set of operations. This provides a simple way to implement security, sharing, and naming of objects.

Whenever an object is accessed, a check is performed against its process list to determine whether it has been opened by the calling process. An object's process list obtains a list of all processes that have opened the object. If the calling process is not found in the process list, the object uses the security ID of the process and performs an open access check. If this call is successful, the object is opened and an entry is made in the object's process list for the calling process.

NT also contains methods for performing security checks when an object is accessed. Suppose someone used a program to monitor the screens of NT workstations over the network. This spy program attempts to simply copy the screens of specific workstations each time the screen changes. When spy attempts to read the pixels displayed on each NT screen, NT will perform a security check against spy's security model. If this check fails, spy will not be able to retrieve anything.

GAINING ACCESS TO AN NT SYSTEM

A user must log on to an NT system before using any of its resources. The logon process is controlled by the logon DLL. Each time a Windowstation is created, a new Windowstation is created by the logon process to handle the security of the new process. See Chapter 5 for an introduction to the term Windowstation.

If the logon is successful, the logon process creates a unique security ID (SID) to represent the logon. After the logon is complete, the logon process sets the Windowstation's owner to the logon SID. After the logon process has set the owner of the Windowstation, the logon process calls the session manager to actually create the Windowstation.

NT uses a secure password encryption system for managing passwords. See Chapters 5, 6, and 9 for more information about passwords.

LOGGING OFF

The logoff process occurs whenever the user exits explicitly by selecting Logoff from the Program Manager File menu or presses Ctrl+Alt+Del and selects the Logoff option.

A user is also logged off any time the user exits his or her shell or Windows NT. Once a user has logged off, anyone trying to gain interactive access to the workstation must log on.

LOCKING YOUR WORKSTATION

A workstation can be locked by pressing Ctrl+Alt+Del and selecting Lock Workstation. When used during an active session, Ctrl+Alt+Del always calls the NT security subsystem, which will respond by displaying the NT Security dialog.

The Desktop settings in Control Panel can also be used to set up a screen saver that will lock the workstation. Using a screen saver to lock the workstation is handy, because this automates the process when the user leaves the machine idle.

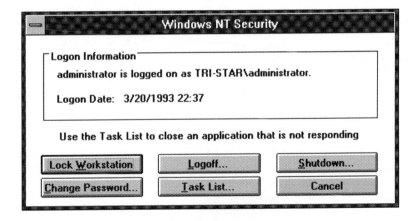

Windows NT Security Dialog

The NT Security dialog displays several bits of information such as your logon time and date and the user who is logged on. The dialog also provides several buttons for taking quick action.

One of the options is Lock Workstation. Click this option and your system is locked until you come back and enter the password to unlock it. The password used to unlock the workstation is the same password used when the user logged on. The administrator for the workstation can also unlock the workstation by using his or her password.

You can also log off, shut down the system, change your password, and select another task from this dialog.

VIRUSES

NT provides a number of features for monitoring and protecting your system against harmful programs such as a virus or a poorly written program. Programs do not have rights in an NT system; thus, they must be executed with the rights of a specific user. Every program executes with the authorization of the user who started the program or the user account that was specified for startup programs in the Services applet. Authenticating programs by user will at worst limit the damage a program can spread on your system. This eliminates back-door entry to the operating system for privileged accounts.

SETTING FILE SYSTEM SECURITY PARAMETERS

NTFS provides a number of security features for controlling and monitoring access to files and directories. These security options are controlled by using the Security menu options. Keep in mind that these options work only on an NTFS volume. Trying to select security options for a non-NTFS volume will generate an error dialog. NTFS security options are covered in detail in Chapter 5.

NT File Security

The Security menu provides access to the security settings for setting permissions on files and directories, setting audit parameters for a file or directory, and taking ownership of a file or directory. Each of these options is explained below.

Security Settings

You can explicitly control who can access your files and what they can do with them by setting permissions on a file or directory. Both groups and users can be granted permissions for files and directories.

NT provides permission options that control whether a user can only read a file, can modify a file, has total access to a file, and so on. The exact permission options are shown in the dialogs presented in this section. See Chapter 5 for the full details of each type of permission.

The following dialog is used to set directory permissions.

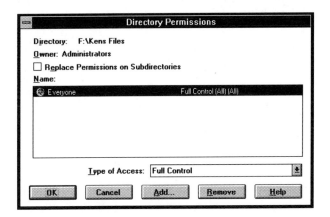

Directory Permissions Dialog

The procedure for setting permissions on a directory or file is very simple:

1. Select the file or directory on which to set permissions.

2. Select Security/Permissions or click the security toolbar button.

3. Complete the process by choosing the users/groups and permissions.

The dialog above has two groups and one user that are granted access to files in this directory structure. The right column shows the type of access granted to the group. The selections in double parentheses show the permissions for the directory and files respectively.

This selection list is displayed by clicking the selection arrow when a user or group is highlighted. The types of directory permissions you can assign are covered in Chapter 5.

The Special Access dialog is displayed when you select Special Access from the Type of Access list. The Special Access dialog has options that are similar to the type of access list (Read) and other options that provide more control (Write, Execute). These options are selected by clicking the selection box. Notice that you can also authorize a user or group to take ownership of the file using this dialog.

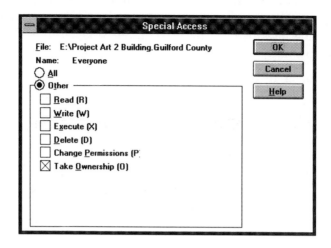

Special Access Dialog

To add a user or group to the permissions list is also very straightforward. Simply click the Add button, and the Add dialog will display a list of groups on your system. The Show Users button will change the display to show user account names in addition to the groups. The user accounts will be displayed together at the end of all groups. You can also select groups or users from another system by using the List Names In drop-down list at the top of the dialog. This list will display a list of network systems from which to select.

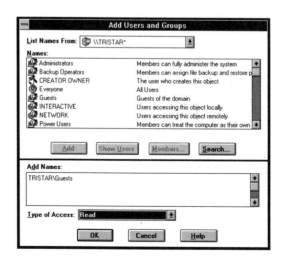

Add Group or User to Permissions Dialog

To add a user or group to the list, click the user/group and click OK or just double-click the user/group. The user/group will be added to the Add Names box at the bottom of the dialog. Multiple users/groups in the Add Names box will be separated by a semicolon (;).

The Search button is a useful feature for finding a user or group across the network. The Search button will display a new dialog that lets you lets you select the user criteria to search for.

The Type of Access list on the bottom of this dialog allows you to change the permissions at this point.

A user or group can be removed from the permissions list by clicking the Remove button with the user or group selected.

Special Directory Access

The Special Directory Access dialog is used to explicitly set permissions on a file or directory.

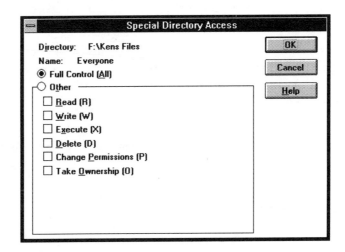

Special Directory Access Dialog

Special Access permissions can be customized by selecting options from this dialog. The options on this dialog are more explicit than the standard directory/file permissions (Execute instead of simply Read) and can give you more control over file and directory resources. If you need explicit control via the Special Access permissions, consult your NT documentation and make sure you completely understand the security permissions for NT files and directories.

Security on Shared Resources

NT supports four permissions on shared resources: No Access, Read, Change, and Full Control. These permissions are similar to the permissions for files. The permissions can be placed on any shared resource, regardless of the file system used by the resource. The permissions are described in the following table.

Permisssion	Description
No Access	The user has no access to the resource.
Read	Read allows a user to display directory names and file names, display data in files, display a file's attributes, run an executable program, run executable files, and change to subdirectories on the shared resource.
Change	The change permission allows a user to perform all the operations of the Read permission, plus create new subdirectories and files, change a file's attributes, change data in the file, append data to the file, and delete the file.
Full Control	The Full Control permission allows a user to perform any action on a file or directory.

Permissions for shared resources are managed by selecting the Permissions button on the Share dialog. You can view or manage permissions by selecting a shared resource and clicking Share. Adding and removing permissions operates the same way as the dialogs for File and Directory permissions.

NTFS users should note that share permissions are combined with the NTFS permissions to determine a user's access to a file or directory. The NTFS permissions will always override conflicting share permissions.

Auditing Files and Directories

Introduction to Auditing
NT also allows you to set up auditing criteria for files and directories. File and Directory auditing records entries in the security log whenever an audited event occurs for a selected user or group when the user or group accesses a file or directory that has auditing turned on.

User Manger is used to turn on auditing for the entire system. The Policies/Audit option will allow you to specify which types of events can be audited. Once this step is complete you must select which resources and users will be audited. File Manager and Print Manager must be used to enable auditing on resources and users.

The Security/Auditing option in File Manager and Print Manager is used to select files and directories or printers for auditing. The menu also has options for setting permissions and taking ownership of a resource.

Once you have selected the resource to audit and checked the events to be audited, NT will begin to log events that meet those criteria in the Security Log. You can use Event Viewer to quickly view the Security Log and search for matching events.

Selecting Objects and Users to Audit
The auditing system allows you to be selective in establishing audit criteria for an NT directory or file. Setting up audit criteria is very similar to setting permissions:

1. Select the file, directories, and printers to audit.

2. Select who should be audited.

3. Select the events to audit.

4. Check the replace box if you want to replace auditing for existing files and directories.

5. Click OK.

The Directory Auditing dialog is shown below. This dialog is shown when you select Security/Auditing with a directory selected. This same dialog is used for selecting audit options for files, except the title is changed to File Auditing.

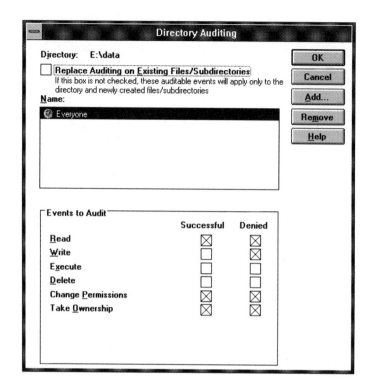

Directory Auditing Dialog

The Replace Auditing check box at the top of the dialog allows you to replace the audit settings for all files and subdirectories. This is useful if you want to clear auditing for an entire drive or directory structure or if you wish to establish new audit settings for an entire structure.

Selecting the Security/Audit option with a file highlighted will display the File Auditing dialog. This dialog allows you to select the events you wish to audit for the file and the users or groups that should be monitored.

The following dialog is the Add Users and Groups dialog for selecting which users to audit for a file. This dialog is identical to the Add dialog from the permissions section. Many NT dialogs for selecting common objects such as users or computers are used by different applications, in the same manner that Windows V3.x provides common dialogs for many services such as selecting files or fonts. Using common dialogs makes using and learning NT much easier.

Notice the options for INTERACTIVE and NETWORK groups in the Add Users and Groups dialog. These options allow you to select the users to audit by how they access the system, either locally or over the network. This is a handy way to track who is using sensitive files on your system.

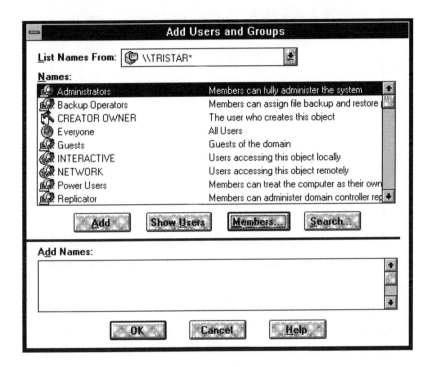

Auditing Add Users and Groups Dialog

Auditing Printers

The Print Manager Security/Auditing menu option is similar to the Auditing option in File Manager. Auditing allows you to select users to monitor for either success or failure for a particular printer. The following figure shows the Printer Auditing dialog for the HP LaserJet III printer.

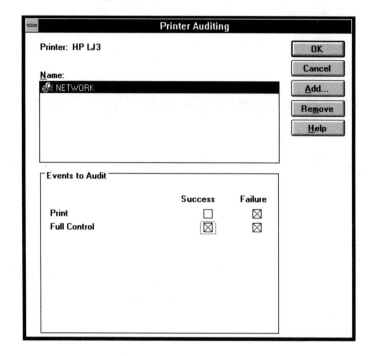

Printer Auditing Dialog

Notice that we have turned on auditing for network users only. This example will trap events for all network users that have trouble printing and any network user that changes anything about a printer or document.

This dialog works exactly like the File Manager Audit dialog for adding or removing users in the audit list.

FILE OWNERSHIP

NTFS tracks the owner of a file or directory when it is created. The owner of a file or directory has complete control over permissions and actions relating to the file or directory. Owners can add or remove permissions as they see fit. Even if an administrator changes the permissions on a file, the owner can change them back.

This system works well in most cases but causes a minor problem when the owner of a group of files or directories leaves a company. NTFS overcomes this by allowing anyone in the Administrators group to take ownership of a file or directory.

The Owner dialog is accessed by the File Manager Security menu option called Owner option. Their are dialogs for single selections (one directory or file) and another for multiple selections. The figure below shows the single-selection Owner dialog. Notice that the owner of the file or directory is shown, along with the file or directory name.

Owner Dialog for a Directory

You can complete the process at this point by clicking on Take Ownership. Clicking on Take Ownership when a directory is selected will display another dialog warning you that all the permissions on files and subdirectories under the selected directory will be changed, giving you full permission. Click OK if you are sure, or click cancel to abort the task.

The figure below shows the Owner dialog for multiple files or directories. This example indicates that there are three files or directories selected but does not show the owner name or the file names.

Owner Dialog for a Group of Files

You can take ownership of the selected files or directories by clicking the Take Ownership button on the dialog.

Transferring ownership of a file or directory from a user who has left the company to another user is a three-step process. First, a member of the Administrators group must take ownership of the file or directory. Second, the new owner of the file or directory must be given Take Ownership privileges. Third, the new owner must perform the Take Ownership process.

PRINTER SECURITY

Setting Printer Permissions

Printer resources are treated similar to files in an NT system. They have security attributes and many other control features. Let's take a brief look at the security features of printers on an NT system.

Printers can have the following permissions:

Permission	Description
No Access	No access to the printer.
Print	Print documents only.
Manage Documents	Control document settings, delete, pause, resume, and restart documents. Does not include print permission.
Full Control	Control all aspects of the printer and documents.

The Printer Permissions dialog is shown below. This dialog is displayed by selecting Permissions form the Security menu.

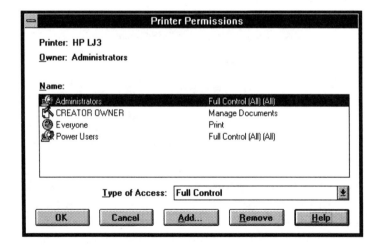

Printer Permissions Dialog

Printer Ownership

Printers have owners exactly like files and directories. The Owner option displays the same Owner dialog as the one in File Manager.

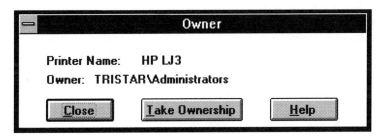

Owner Dialog

Click the Take Ownership button to take ownership of the printer.

POLICIES

Policies are another feature that NT provides for managing a system. Policies are rules that provide basic guidelines for certain aspects of a system. Accounts, User Rights, and Audit procedures use policies to control how they function. For instance, the Accounts policy controls the defaults for how passwords are managed and what happens when passwords are changed.

Policies can be changed by the administrator of an NT workstation. Before making any changes you should review the defaults installed with NT, because they are fairly complete for most systems.

RIGHTS

NT uses rights to define what actions a user may perform on the system. Rights apply to the entire system and do not apply to specific objects such as files, directories, or printers.

Rights will always take precedence over permissions. For instance, if a user has an account on a system but does not have the right to access this computer over the network, that user will not be able to gain access to the system over the network. The user may be able to log in locally but will be blocked from network access because he or she lacks the right.

A full discussion of user rights is outside the scope of this book. If your system is in a very secure environment, you should consult the NT documentation on rights and experiment with rights on a nonsecure system.

Index

W •

X •

Also Available from CBM Books

BOOKS

VAX I/O Subsystems: Optimizing Performance by Ken Bates	$49	1-878956-02-7
Introduction to VAX/VMS, 3rd Edition by David W. Bynon and Terry C. Shannon	$35	1-878956-05-1
VMS Advanced Device Driver Techniques by Jamie E. Hanrahan and Lee Leahy	$60	0-9614729-5-2
Mastering VMS by David W. Bynon	$40	0-9614729-7-9
The Open Desktop Companion: A Guide for *PC and Workstation Users* by David W. Bynon	$28	1-878956-23-X
VMS Performance Management by James W. Coburn	$30	1-878956-21-3
The Hitchhiker's Guide to VMS by Bruce Ellis	$35	1-878956-00-0
A Manager's Guide to Multivendor Networks by John Enck	$35	1-878956-03-5
UNIX, Quick! by Andrew Feibus	$30	1-878956-01-9
Introduction to Data Communications: *A Practical Approach* by Stan Gelber	$39	1-878956-04-3
The Dictionary of Standard C by Rex Jaeschke	$17	1-878956-07-8
Mastering Standard C: A Self-Paced Training *Course in Modern C* by Rex Jaeschke	$40	0-9614729-8-7
Portability & the C Language by Rex Jaeschke	$19	0-672-48428-5
C++: An Introduction for Experienced C Programmers by Rex Jaeschke	$30	1-878956-27-2
Data Communications & Networking Dictionary by T.D. Pardoe and R.P. Wenig	$24	1-878956-06-X
PC Power: A Guide to DOS and Windows Systems *for Computer-Literate Users* by David S. Quimby	$19	1-878956-30-2
Ethernet Pocket Guide: A Practical Guide to Designing, *Installing, and Troubleshooting Ethernet Networks* by Byron Spinney	$15	1-878956-25-6
The Complete Guide to PATHWORKS: PATHWORKS *for VMS and DOS* (disk included) by Ken Spencer	$39	1-878956-22-1
Navigating the AS/400: A Hands-On Guide by John Enck and Michael Ryan	$39	1-878956-31-0

VIDEOTAPES AND KITS

Desktop Systems Integrator Kit (disk included) by Al Cini	$49	1-878956-28-0
The Hitchhiker's Guide to VMS Performance Part I: VMS Memory Management and Paging Performance (1 tape/1 study guide) with Bruce Ellis	$499	1-878956-09-4
The Hitchhiker's Guide to VMS Performance Part II: I/0 Performance (1 tape, 1 study guide) with Bruce Ellis	$499	1-878956-12-4
The Hitchhiker's Guide to VMS Performance Part III: CPU Performance (1 tape, 1 study guide) with Bruce Ellis	$499	1-878956-15-9
How They'll Hack Your VAX, and How to Prevent It (2 tapes, 1 study guide) with Bruce Ellis	$599	1-878956-18-3

Available at your bookstore or, in the U.S., order by phone: (215) 957-4265.
Prices subject to change.

CBM Books

VAX I/0 Subsystems: Optimizing Performance by Ken Bates

Learn how to analyze and improve I/O performance from leading expert Ken Bates, a member of the original development teams for both the HSC and KDM70 controllers, and the developer of the first striping product offered by Digital.

"(This book) explores the right strategies to help system managers obtain the greatest total performance from their systems."
— Grant Saviers, Vice President, PC & Systems Peripherals Group, Digital Equipment Corporation

"A landmark book."
— DEC Professional

1-878956-02-7/$49

Mastering VMS by David W. Bynon

This handbook uses step-by-step examples and explanations on how to apply VMS system operation and management techniques. Hands-on instruction for system managers, programmers, operators and analysts.

"Provides the reader with information on everything from the rise of the VAX machine and study of the VMS operating system to information on VMS operation management, utilities and commands."
— The Office

"A valuable book for those using the VMS operating system."
— CHOICE

0-9614729-7-9/$40

The Open Desktop Companion: A Guide for PC and Workstation Users by David W. Bynon

A must-have, easy-to-use guide to the Open Desktop graphical user interface, Open Desktop DOS, the underlying SCO UNIX operating system and Open Desktop's networking capabilities.

"This handsomely presented technical volume will have most value to system administrators as well as sophisticated and committed end users."
— Small Press

1-878956-23-X/$28

VMS Performance Management by James W. Coburn

With in-depth discussions of VMS tuning, this book includes a wealth of information that goes beyond the Digital manuals. It describes techniques for analyzing VMS systems and correcting performance-related problems.

"VMS tuning methods are thought by many to border on the mystical. Mr. Coburn dispels that myth. His concise, easy-to-follow examination of VMS performance management reduces system tuning to a level approachable by mere mortals — or system managers."

— *DEC Professional*

1-878956-21-3/$30

The Hitchhiker's Guide to VMS by Bruce Ellis

This unusual programmer's guide from VMS internals guru Bruce Ellis transforms hands-on system programming tips into a fast, fun read. From VMS internals and process concepts to system data structures and security, *The Hitchhiker's Guide to VMS* covers all the bases.

"Bruce Ellis is the only author I've found who can write entertainingly about the low-level details of VMS. The book is amazingly fun to read…you'll learn a lot."

— *DECUSCOPE*

"… put your thumb up, this hitchhike could be the most enjoyable learning experience you've had."

— *ON$DECK Magazine*

1-878956-00-0/$35

A Manager's Guide to Multivendor Networks by John Enck

This book defines fundamental network architectures and explores the standards, topologies and technologies that affect multivendor networking and data communications strategies.

"Without reading like alphabet soup, (A Manager's Guide to Multivendor Networks) rounds up the key functions, services and equipment that managers must grasp conceptually to spearhead successful networking projects."

— *Computerworld*

"A Manager's Guide to Multivendor Networks takes a simple approach to a complex subject. It is recommended reading for anyone desiring a block-diagram look at network implementation."

— *Workstation*

1-878956-03-5/$35

UNIX, Quick! by Andrew Feibus

It doesn't get much easier than these shortcuts and simple techniques for learning the UNIX operating system fast. Step-by-step instructions show you how to use basic functions and features and more advanced techniques.

"Andrew Feibus' book aims to give DOS users a trouble-free transition to UNIX by cutting out unnecessary commands, procedures and utilities."

— *IBM Computer Today*

1-878956-01-9/$30

Introduction to Data Communications: A Practical Approach by Stan Gelber

For systems analysts, programmers, engineers, customer service reps, sales support personnel, mid-level managers... anyone whose job requires knowing and understanding data communications concepts and applications.

"(Author Stan Gelber) skillfully uses his extensive experience to provide very detailed, useful, hands-on information for the MIS professional and systems analyst building corporate networks... His understanding of the public telephone network and equipment that interfaces to it to provide corporations with a variety of capabilities is unmatched in the literature."

— *LAN Computing*

1-878956-04-3/$39

The Dictionary of Standard C by Rex Jaeschke

C guru Rex Jaeschke has written the only comprehensive resource defining the terminology of the C language.

"Rex Jaeschke's books have always focused on making the C language more accessible and understandable to all C programmers. The Dictionary of Standard C continues this tradition by providing clear, concise definitions for the many concepts and technical terms with which both novice and experienced programmers should be familiar."

— Jim Brodie, Chair of ANSI C Standards Committee X3J11

"I would recommend this indispensable book to students and C programmers...it is equally valuable as a complete C language reference."

— Wilson Mbakweni, *Computing*

1-878956-07-8/$17

Mastering Standard C: A Self-Paced Training Course in Modern C by Rex Jaeschke

A self-teaching workbook on the statements and constructs of the C language written by Rex Jaeschke, internationally acclaimed C expert and voting member of the ANSI C Standards Committee X3J11.

"If you want to learn the C language and are willing to spend some time learning it end to end, Mastering Standard C *is a good way to go."*

— *Dr. Dobb's Journal*

0-9614729-8-7/$40

Data Communications & Networking Dictionary by T.D. Pardoe and R.P. Wenig

This book provides definitions for communications and networking terms ranging from the most basic to the most complex — a useful learning aid for beginners and a valuable reference for experts. Over 2,000 listings define networking standards, acronyms, and common abbreviations of communications and networking terms.

"If you need help understanding the difference between a bridge, a hub and a router, this dictionary deserves a place on your bookshelf."

— *Engineering Automation Report*

1-878956-06-X/$24

Available at your bookstore. Or, in the U.S., call to order: (215) 957-4265

Other CBM Books' Titles

A Practical Guide to Windows NT

Kenneth L. Spencer
$25
Softcover, 217 pages

MIS personnel and end-users alike will find this guide an indispensable resource for understanding Windows NT. Essential reading for anyone interested in the future of computing.

The Complete Guide to PATHWORKS: PATHWORKS for VMS and DOS

3 1/2" disk included

Kenneth L. Spencer
$39
Softcover, 390 pages

Explains how to implement a PATHWORKS LAN. Put a copy on every network manager's desk. Helpful for all MIS staff — and even end users.

PC Power: A Guide to DOS and Windows Systems for Computer-Literate Users

David S. Quimby
$19
Softcover, 250 pages

Stepping from midranges and mainframes to PCs can be disorienting unless you have the power. Read PC Power and get up to speed in DOS and Windows on PCs.

TP Software Development for OpenVMS

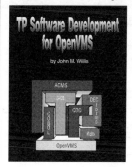

John M. Willis
$35
Softcover, 360 pages.

Digital's Transaction Processing (TP) software is explained in a practical, hands-on manner. Programmers, analysts and project managers will benefit.

C++: An Introduction for Experienced C Programmers

Rex Jaeschke
$30
Softcover, 240 pages

A fast and easy introduction into C++ for those who know their way around C. This self-training tool includes C++ problems you're likely to encounter — and their step by step solutions.

To order, complete the reverse side and mail or. . .

FOR FASTER SERVICE. . .
Phone (215) 957-4265
FAX (215) 957-1050
Through CompuServe User ID
76702,1565

CBM
BOOKS

Satisfaction Guaranteed!

CBM Books Order Form

CBM BOOKS

For fast, easy ordering . . .
- By Phone (215) 957-4265   ■ FAX (215) 957-1050
- Through CompuServe Mail — User ID 76702,1565

Title			Quantity	Subtotal
A Practical Guide to Windows NT 1-5 books		$25.00 each		
6-15 books	SAVE 15%!	$21.25 each		
16-49 books	SAVE 30%!	$17.50 each		
50 + books	SAVE 40%!	$15.00 each		
The Complete Guide to PATHWORKS: PATHWORKS for VMS and DOS		$39		
PC Power: A Guide to DOS and Windows Systems for Computer-Literate Users		$19		
TP Software Development for OpenVMS		$35		
C++: An Introduction for Experienced C Programmers		$30		
PA residents add 6% sales tax.				
UPS shipping: In the U.S., $4 for the first book, $1 for each additional book. Outside the U.S., please call (215) 957-4265 for shipping information.				
TOTAL ORDER				

Name _____

Title _____

Company _____

Street Address (required) _____

City _____ State _____ Zip _____

Country _____

Telephone (_____) _____ FAX (_____) _____

☐ Payment enclosed $_____ (payable to Cardinal Business Media, Inc.)

Charge to: ☐ MasterCard   ☐ VISA   ☐ American Express

Account #: _____ Exp. Date _____

Signature _____ Date _____

☐ **Please send me a FREE catalog.**

Mail to: **CBM Books**
101 Witmer Road
P.O. Box 446
Horsham, PA 19044

Satisfaction Guaranteed!

CBM Books Money Back Guarantee: CBM guarantees all of its books. If you are not completely satisfied with your selection for any reason, return it within 30 days for a refund of the full purchase price.

WNTB0893